Pooped Doggy

Pooped Doggy

Arthur Graves

iUniverse, Inc.
New York Lincoln Shanghai

Pooped Doggy

iUniverse, Inc.

For information address:
iUniverse, Inc.
2021 Pine Lake Road, Suite 100
Lincoln, NE 68512
www.iuniverse.com

ISBN: 0-595-33808-9

Printed in the United States of America

"To my family…the driving force behind all I do."

February 26, 2004

The Span of Life

"The old dog barks backward without getting up.

I can remember when he was a pup."

Robert Frost

This seemed a fitting post for a day I celebrate turning 34. It is probably the only poem, with the exception of a few Ogden Nash quips, that I can recite from memory. My Dad would spit this little ditty out every so often, and it must have stuck. I never really thought much about what it meant, but on a day that I am "getting older"; I can see what Frost was getting at.

Everyone who has been lucky enough to have a furry friend growing up can picture the old dog hearing something and looking back over his shoulder to see what's going on. He's interested, but age (and maybe experience) prevents him from hopping up and running over, tail wagging, to investigate. The person watching him sees this process and fondly remembers the days when the old guy would just react, playful and cheery, and run over without thinking.

The dog isn't old in the sense of being arthritic and immobile. I get the impression he's just wiser. With his age, he's come to realize that he doesn't need to get all worked up about things that happen on a daily basis. He still let's you know he's watching. He'll turn around and let out a sharp "woof", as if to say "I'm still here and paying attention".

I'm not one to worry about "growing old". I remember being a "pup" and still feel that light hearted enthusiasm about life. Hey, what's better than to enjoy each day with family and friends and look forward to all the things left to learn and experience.

March 02, 2004

Not So Super Tuesday

Today is the day the Democrats will likely solidify their choice of a candidate to oppose George Bush this fall. The story doesn't seem too exciting. It appears the only real question mark is whether Kerry will sweep the day or not. But, in politics you never know. Just ask Howard Dean. YEEEEEEOOOOOUUUUUC-CCHHHHH!

In the past, I was much more hyped on primary days. I loved to debate just about any issue, for fun, for the challenge, and for principle. This year, this bunch rubs me wrong. They all seem to be the same guy in different suits. I don't know what any of them really think about the issues, other than the fact that it's the opposite of what George Bush thinks.

So, being unenthused about the goings on of the day, I thought I'd take the opportunity to make an observation on politics itself rather than the politicians.

My senior year at St. Lawrence, I was required to write a thesis as part of my Philosophy degree. It wasn't a real thesis. I didn't have to devote a year of my life researching to create a 200 page, bound masterpiece. Our "thesis" was really a semester long project on a philosophy or philosopher that we had some interest in. I chose The Prince, by Niccolo Machiavelli.

The reasons for my choice were two fold, one based on principle and a belief in a school of thought, and the other as a rebellious (OK, petty) gesture toward all the "wanna be" philosophers in my class. There were more than a handful of students who spent that semester determining whether or not the chair I sat on "really existed" or whether the color green was really green to everyone. It was really fun sitting in on those presentations.

I chose Machiavelli because he is likely the most misunderstood philosopher in history. His philosophy is not abstract; it's practical, almost scientific.

The Prince gives a clear description of how to seize and maintain political power. It has been labeled as ruthless, immoral, harsh, etc. Need I say more? This gets back to the petty thing…I partly chose it to annoy the "touchy feelies" in class.

After reading the text, however, I soon began to realize it wasn't harsh or ruthless; it was realistic. This book was not meant to be "political." If you wanted to gain control and keep in control, this book gave you an historical account of successful and unsuccessful ways of achieving this goal.

I know, I know, I'm rambling. It's a long way to get to Super Tuesday. However, Machiavelli felt there were two key factors for any leader to be successful, Opportunity and Fortune. Opportunity is being in the right place at the right time. It's having the experience, qualifications, money, etc. at the point in time when political power is up for grabs.

Fortune is a little tougher to define. It is circumstance; the things that arise and cannot be planned for. A leader needs to always be ready to react. Once a leader begins to "rest on his laurels," he is open to potential pitfalls. Machiavelli likened fortune to a raging river during a flood, sweeping away trees and buildings, destroying whatever crosses it's path. However, when the weather turns fair, defenses can be made. Dams can be constructed and canals can be built to channel the water and not allow its force to be so unrestrained and dangerous. A good leader, likewise, prepares as best as possible for the unexpected.

So today on Super Tuesday, it appears that John Kerry will wrap up the Democratic nomination. Should he then give his acceptance speech, kick back and relax? For that matter, should President Bush wait things out? Assess the situation and wait to act?

Not if either has learned from The Prince. Fortune *will* change things. Who is going to be able to adjust the best?

George Bush has established his ability to tackle fortune. The events of 9/11 demanded the President act. His ability to handle the situation was reflected in soaring approval ratings. My money is on W. to come through again. Besides, he's a sure thing to pick up *all* the Republican delegates today on Super Tuesday!

March 03, 2004

The Uncarved Block

As I was watching (and listening to) John Kerry speak last night, my mind started to wander. He continues to talk about the gap between the haves and have-nots, and how it is expanding. Usually this speech is being conducted while he is "hanging with a bunch of regular guys."

It strikes me just how hard he is trying to appear like a typical guy. His net worth is calculated using more zeros than cows in Vermont, yet he acts like he's one of us. Why is this so apparent to me? Am I looking for it, or do others see this as well?

Maybe it's obvious because he seems so unnatural. His appearances are labored; trying to fulfill the image of who he'd like to be, rather than who he is. Heck, the guy even calls himself the second JFK from Massachusetts.

There is a Taoist principle called the Uncarved Block. It states that all things have a certain natural power in their original form. Call it your "natural state" or "inner self." In simple terms, when you are truly yourself, you're at your best.

People in the state of the Uncarved Block are in touch with themselves. Life is simple and enjoyable. There isn't wasted time and stress trying to "be something" they're not.

In case you didn't know, I like the President. Yes, ideologically we are similar, but I think that alone isn't it. I trust him, and I get the feeling he means everything he says. People may not agree with him, but he has opinions and beliefs that are firm and principled. He's got a bit of cowboy in him, and it shows at times. He doesn't pretend to be a scholar; just a leader that does what he thinks is best. I recognize that he has faults, and you don't get to the Presidency without being at least partly political, but I do respect the fact that he's a straight shooter.

It's too bad that Howard Dean was ousted in the past few weeks. I could not be any further philosophically from Dean, however I enjoyed having him around. He, like Bush, was himself. Raw and uncensored, he often spoke before he thought, which probably hurt him some, but also endeared him to so many who are tired of the polished, professional politicians.

So, now we're down to two remaining (oh yeah, three. I almost forgot about Mr. Nader) until Election Day. I think it's going to be a long eights months. Like Chris Matthews said, "you can have a baby in that time!"

However, I think over the course of the summer, we'll start to see someone distinguish themselves from the rest. History has shown us that no matter how close a first term Presidential election was, re-elections are typically not nail bit-ers. The TV pundits are already displaying their computerized state maps and detailing every possible electoral scenario.

Come Election Day in November, I believe we won't be on the edge of our chair at 2:00am waiting for some clue as to who will lead our country. I think the people will lean toward a leader they read as genuine.

A cowboy doesn't stick his finger in the air to determine which way to head next. He trusts his heart.

March 09, 2004

Fisher Excitement

Late last week as Nora and I were going through our morning routine before heading off for school, some movement caught my eye in our backyard. I have a tendency, or as Kelly calls it, a neurosis, to regularly look into the woods for signs of wildlife. On the rare occasion I actually see something, it is generally followed by a frantic attempt to inform Kelly of the "sighting."

The woods start just before an old stonewall intended to mark the edge of our property. Pine and Poplar are mixed throughout, with the occasional young maple straining for its share of sunlight. On that morning, several days of high winds left a speckled blanket of pine needles atop the snow bed, making it difficult to see the wall in the early morning light. It was just past this stonewall where I experienced my most recent sighting.

Our neighborhood is filled with big dogs, mostly labs, that like to wander through everyone's yard but their own, I assume in an attempt to help keep everyone's grass green. So naturally, I thought it was likely either Toby or Chewy out for a walk. But a second glance confirmed it was not. My visitor was a touch smaller, black, and running with a funny gait. Its butt-end (long tail included) was much higher than its head and shoulders. It wasn't moving quickly, but it wasn't loafing either. I watched it walk parallel to the house for maybe 10 seconds before it moved out of sight.

"Kelly!" *(Yelling)*

Of course, Kelly had already left for work. What was I going to do now? Who could I share this excitement with?

"Da Da Da Da Da."

Nora was playing with the string on her pants when she blurted her favorite string of sounds. I like to think she was calling me by name, but she tends to say that whenever she gets excited (including when I'm not even home).

"Nora, look what Daddy saw!" I picked her up and we both looked out the window, searching. No more movement.

"Da Da Da Da Da!" Nora burst, with an excitement that caught me by surprise.

"What is it Nora?"

She reached out her little hand as if to point out into the woods. This is great! She's just like her Daddy! As her hand reached the window, she grabbed hold of the lock lever and began to try to move it back and forth. With each attempt, she'd look at me and laugh, with that proud look of someone who has just made a wonderful discovery. This is what she thought was interesting.

I think Nora and I had a bonding experience and she taught me something special that morning. I know how excited I felt when I saw something unusual. The first thing I wanted to do was to share it with someone close to me. I hope that there are more things than not that still excite me, things I want to share with others. As I "grow up," it seems so much easier to overlook all the interesting things right in front of us. Wouldn't it be wonderful to be able to feel the excitement Nora showed me when she saw a window lock for the first time? Not long before that, a Tupperware bowl, a measuring cup and the remote control were the excitement of the day. Everything she sees is new, and she is learning from it all.

Her enthusiasm is contagious, and I for one, have caught her bug.

Note: I believe what I saw was a fisher. Bailey and I went "hunting" that night, but could find no tracks or signs of the critter.

March 12, 2004

Writer's Block

Typically, I have no trouble deciding on a topic to write about. Enough happens each day to set my mind spinning, and experiences turn to ideas. However, on the odd occasion, I find myself laboring for inspiration. The words don't seem to flow, and what I manage to get on paper is either boring or not of the quality I strive for. I suppose all writer's go through this at some point.

When I decided to start this blog, my intent was to simply use the space as my sounding board. To some degree I liked the idea that others may read what I write, but I mostly wanted to practice putting my thoughts into words. Unlike McDonald's Super Size fries, this is a case where more is better. With each post, I become more comfortable with my style.

At dinner last night, I asked Kelly for some food for thought, in the hopes of coming up with something to write about. Without hesitation, she jovially suggested I write an "Ode to My Wife." Not that it was a bad idea, but how can I wrap that into an engaging story? Our conversation drifted back to the day's tribulations at work and plans for the weekend. Soon it was time to feed Nora her peas and head to bed for the night.

This morning I woke quite refreshed for my morning run. I hopped on the treadmill and turned on the news to see if anything other than the terror attack in Spain was being covered. Nope. One thought kept racing through my mind, an *Ode to My Wife!*

What is an *ode*, anyway? Poetry? I can handle that:

The hornet in orange and black,

Caught my eye while running the track.

Where do I start?

She captured my heart.

I made the right choice, looking back.

OK, maybe that's not really what she meant by an ode! But I think it captures the *spirit* of an ode. It's hard to believe, but we met more than 17 years ago. What seemed like a high school crush at the time, laid the foundation for our family today.

In my worries about what to right in my blog today, I overlooked the fact that tonight (the Friday before St. Patrick's Day) marks the anniversary of the day I proposed to that girl I first met on a trip to Buffalo. In some ways it seems like yesterday, although seven years have past. That night we went to dinner, ate a huge dessert (she can't pass up a Butcher Block brownie sundae), and I asked her to marry me in the room we spent so much time in as high school sweethearts.

Now I can say I've written my first ode. I think it's also safe to say that I've worked through my writer's block. Kelly didn't realize it at the time, but she gave me the perfect subject matter to work with.

For that matter, back in high school she didn't realize at the time that she was giving me a whole lot more.

March 15, 2004

The Ides of March

"Beware the Ides of March."

We've all heard this warning, given to Julius Caesar by a soothsayer (fortune-teller) shortly before his assassination. Although we've heard it, does it mean anything? Other than the fact that it marked the day Caesar was assassinated, I never really knew what the Ides of March was.

William Shakespeare wrote of the encounter Caesar had with the soothsayer. The man shouted a warning and caught Caesar's attention. Caesar was curious at first, and asked the man to approach him, so he could study his face. Satisfied that the comment was not a concern, Caesar replied to the prophecy, "He is a dreamer; let us leave him."

We now know that Caesar made the wrong choice.

Why didn't Caesar take the man seriously? By some accounts he did. I've learned that according to the Roman calendar, the ides fall on the 15th of March, May, July and October. All other months the ides fall on the 13th. Yes, that means there's an ides of April, and May, and June, etc. The Romans didn't call each day by number. For example, March 11 was called "IV (four) ides," or four days before the ides of March. All other days of the month are named in relation to either the Kalends (1st day of the month) or the Nones (the 7th day in March, May, July, and October; the 5th in the other months). As you can see, it may be quite easy to be off a day!

Could it be possible Caesar just forgot the month? In Shakespeare's writing, there may be support for this. Caesar had a second encounter with the soothsayer in which he told him "The ides of March have come." Caesar obviously thought he was in the clear, as he made a point to tell the soothsayer he was wrong. The soothsayer, however, coyly replied, "Ay, Caesar, but not gone." It was his way of saying the day was not done.

We likely will never know if Caesar simply dismissed the soothsayer as a crackpot, or if he let his guard down, as he thought the day of the prophetic warning had passed.

By now, you're probably wondering why the heck I'm writing about this. As I was lying in bed this morning, shutting off the alarm for the third time, I realized I was not going to have the gumption to get my workout in. In a lame attempt at humor (give me a break, it was 6:00 am!), I said to myself, "Great! The Ides of

March!" Ok, I'm a geek, but it was something to blame not running on other than my laziness.

For those of you interested, the Boston Marathon is five weeks from today. A check of the Boston Website earlier today showed that 19,255 runners were registered. That's fast approaching the cap of 20,000. I believe I've done a better job in preparation for this race than any other in my running career. I've done the long runs, tempo runs, a few races, and I think I have the right mental focus this time around. This morning was a deserved day off, and I'm not going to kick myself around for sleeping in.

Come April 19th, or as the Romans say, come "XII Kalends May" I'll be ready.

March 17, 2004

The Orange and The Green

Oh, it is the biggest mix-up that you have ever seen.

My father, he was Orange and me mother, she was green.

My father was an Ulster man, proud Protestant was he.

My mother was a Catholic girl, from county Cork was she.

They were married in two churches, lived happily enough,

Until the day that I was born and things got rather tough.

Oh, it is the biggest mix-up that you have ever seen.

My father, he was Orange and me mother, she was green.

I remember singing this old Irish rebel song each year in music class as St. Patrick's Day approached. The above is the limit of my memory of the lyrics, so I tend to repeat the same few lines over and over throughout the day. The song was performed, and written I presume, by the Irish Rovers.

As we all know, religion in Ireland is a pretty serious matter. The country is split geographically into the North and South, and this split is mostly a result of religious preference. The North is predominantly Protestant (represented by the color Orange) and the South is predominantly Catholic (represented by the color green). This song is one of the few that poke fun at religious differences on the Emerald Isle.

The song is actually quite relevant to my family, however backwards. My Mom was brought up Protestant and my Dad, Catholic. In our case, it may have led to a few interesting conversations, but never any "big mix-ups."

Irish blood runs in both our families, and we take a certain amount of pride in that. So, it is natural that a traditional meal and some good conversation be the centerpiece for celebrating this day. In that vein, we plan to head to my parent's house tonight for corned beef, cabbage, soda bread, and maybe a pint or two. (Note: Kelly's *traditional meal* may actually be a veggie burger to replace the corned beef.)

The conversation tonight will likely surround Nora, and the arrival of her first two teeth. Although she is shy about sharing them with people, her fussiness and fever have clearly announced the presence of her new "choppers".

The subject of our trip to Ireland, now 5 years ago, will also likely come up. It remains as the most enjoyable vacation I've had, and one I long to revisit at some point in the future. We spent 10 days traveling the southern half of Ireland, from Dublin to Galway, and eventually back to Dublin. We saw Waterford, Kilkenny, Cork, Blarney, Kinsale, The Cliffs of Moher, and New Grange. And yes, we were in Ireland on St. Patrick's Day!

The day (March 17, 1999) started in Blarney. We had traveled to Blarney from Cahir the night before, where we had spent the night at Carageen Castle. As the Irish would say, we rose to a "lovely" day, sunny and warm. We wanted to get an early start, as we were headed to Blarney Castle. We were among the first there, and leisurely climbed the narrow, steep, stone stairway to the top of the castle in anticipation of facing the famed Blarney Stone. As the story goes, all those who kiss the stone are granted the gift of eloquence.

Sounds easy, huh? Oh no! To kiss this stone, you have to lie down, lean back-wards while holding onto an iron railing, and reach your head back over the edge of the castle. Mind you, this is done at a height of roughly 200 feet, with only that rail and a friendly Irish "spotter" preventing you from a sure demise. I quickly kissed the unassuming stone, tossed the spotter a tip and stepped back to photograph Kelly risk her life to join me in my newfound verbal gift. She survived as well. We took a few pictures from atop the castle (one of which hangs in our living room), and decided to leave Blarney.

Our plan was to reach Killarney by early evening, find a bed and breakfast for the night, and get a nice quiet St. Patrick's Day dinner. En route to Killarney we stopped in Kinsale, a very cute, but crowded, port city. We walked through town, shopped a little and ate a magnificent lunch at The Blue Haven Hotel. We ordered a "boxty," which is a traditional potato dish with onions, bacon, and herbs. I washed it down with a Caffrey's Beer and we were on our way to Killarney.

By the time we arrived in Killarney and found a room, it was after 5:00. We were both a bit tired, and decided to take a walk into town to find a quick snack for dinner. We ended up finding a little shop selling green soft serve. And so, we ended our day in Ireland on St. Patrick's Day eating green ice cream on the streets of Killarney.

As we finished our snack and headed back to our room, I remember deciding to call our parents to fill them in on our trip to that point. Kelly called her Mom, and I spoke to my parents. In both cases the conversation was short, just a "Hi, How are you, see you in a few days" kind of thing. But looking back we must have been thinking, like I was when I started this entry, that St. Patrick's Day is about family.

March 19, 2004

Sleep and Racing

I'm in full Boston Marathon countdown mode now! As of this writing, there are 31 days until I toe the line in Hopkinton. This weekend is a key part of my preparation for the marathon. Four weeks out, my last sharpening race is scheduled for tomorrow. I'm hoping for a solid effort and a confidence boost following my aborted effort in the Hudson Mohawk Winter Marathon last month.

For the third consecutive year, I plan to race the Run for Hope 20K. The race starts in Keene, NY at The Elm Tree Inn, a local Adirondack burger joint and ends just past the Cobble Hill Golf Course in Elizabethtown. Billed as a half marathon, the course is actually short of the required 13.1 miles. I've twice clocked the route and found that it is an accurate 20K (12.4 miles).

The course itself is renowned as one of the toughest around, with the first 4 miles climbing out of Keene and up Spruce Hill. A real *quad burner*! The next 8-plus miles are either downhill or flat, with several portions that are quite steep. I've found that my pace averages around 7-minute miles for the first four, and hovering just below 6 minutes for the rest. Two years ago I ran 1:16:01, which is my goal this year.

My training coming in has been consistent. Mentally, I'm ready. But, with this race, and likely with Boston, I'll be testing my ability to adapt to something new. No, I won't be trying a different flavor of Gu, or a new pair of racing flats. *I'm talking about sleep.*

I've never worried about the amount of sleep I get. I'm not one who needs a solid eight hours each night in order to function the next day. Rather, I comfortably get by with 6 or 7 hours. In the past, if I felt tired, I'd just sleep a little later on Saturday and Sunday, catch up, and I'd feel fine.

But, once you have a child, you no longer control your schedule. I've noticed it's more difficult to drag myself out of bed in the morning, and Saturdays and Sundays are no longer available as catch-up days. I'm attempting to adjust, and this weekend will be my first major test. And to really make the test true, Kelly will be working Saturday, so I'll have to rise even a bit earlier to pack-up Nora and all her associated gear to head to Grandma and Grandpa's house for the morning. *(Note: I have not asked if this is an option yet. Some planner I am!)*

Now don't get me wrong, I'm not complaining. It goes without saying that I'd closet my running shoes long before I'd spend less time with my little girl. It is just another adjustment. I'll manage a way to maximize my time with Nora *and* still compete. I just hope that adjustment comes quickly. But if not, I'll revise my goals accordingly.

So, once we put Nora down for the night (around 8:00 pm), I'll hit the sack early myself, right?

Well, there is March Madness!

March 22, 2004

A Ferrari, Gestalt, and Picking Up After Dinner

On my way to work this morning, just as I was getting up to speed on the interstate, a blur of red flashed by before I realized anyone was behind me. As best I could tell, a Ferrari with Quebec plates was the culprit. You don't get to see a Ferrari in Clinton County too often, so this was a relatively momentous event. Although this speedster appeared brand new, I couldn't help being reminded of Cameron's family Ferrari in *Ferris Bueller's Day Off*.

Remember the car they *borrowed* (and ultimately destroyed) to zip around Chicago while playing hooky from school? I was a junior in high school when the movie was in theaters, and everything about it seemed *so* cool. Heck, they even made going to a museum seem like fun! To this day I can correctly identify Seraut's A Sunday on La Grand Jatte.

As a teenager, art didn't appeal to me. But seeing the way the director chose to continually focus in on the little girl in the painting was intriguing. I read a little, and learned that Seraut has been credited as being the founder of pointillism. Very simply, pointillists use tiny dots of complimentary colors to create a picture. Up close, the individual dots are obvious, but take a step back, and all the pieces come together to define an image. In essence, the whole is greater than the sum of its parts. Each little dot itself may seem remote, or unimportant, but taken as part of the entire image it becomes indispensable.

This concept has crossed from art to psychology. Gestalt therapy also holds that the whole is greater than the sum of its parts. A person is defined by experiences and relationships in their past. Individually, the experiences add little, but taken as a whole, shape whom a person is.

Gestalt therapy holds two ideas at its core. The first is that it emphasizes the "here and now." The focus of therapy should be on the experiential present. The second is that we are shaped by our relationship to everything around us.

The philosophy behind Gestalt therapy recognizes that our past has a role in who we are, but it doesn't get stuck working in the past. Patients are taught the difference between talking about what occurred five minutes ago (or last night, or 20 years ago) and *experiencing* what is *now*.

I'm an amateur, and this is only my interpretation/opinion. I'm not going to set up a booth a la Lucy and counsel.

I started thinking about this today as I listened to Imus discuss with Tom Friedman the assassination of Hamas founder Ahmed Yassin. It may be a stretch, but these two opposing sides (Israel and Palestine) have been killing each other for years based on events that happened decades ago. Likewise in our country with racial issues, some people believe they are entitled to benefits based on how previous generations were treated.

At some point we need to understand that the past shapes who we are, and may even lead us down a certain path. However, how you act *today* is your choice. Carrying hate from generation to generation is not productive. If the energy and effort spent on the destruction of the opposition were channeled to an honest understanding of the perspective "on the other side of the fence," the results would likely be remarkable.

Granted, at times I look at the world with utopian eyes. Heck, I *still* have a hard time cleaning off my plate and putting it in the dishwasher after dinner, and not just piling it in the sink. If I can't fix these little behavioral problems, how can I expect the world to change?

I guess I work on what I can control.

Tonight, I'll load the dishwasher.

March 30, 2004

Shake It Like A Polaroid Picture

I drink a lot of Pepsi. And no, that's not an exaggeration. If you want a visual representation of my soda consumption, just take a peek at the floor of the passenger side of my car. The mound is sufficiently high to prevent use of the door, for fear of an avalanche of bottles.

I admit, it's a vice, the only real vice I have. I don't need to drink soda, I just *really* like it! How bad does that sound? What is that first stage of admitting you have a problem? (Insert bad joke here)

You know, de Nile ain't just a river in Egypt!

All kidding aside, I don't really have a *problem* with drinking soda, any more than I have an affinity for eating entire "party-sized" bags of M&Ms in a sitting. When I started running, I needed to lose a significant amount of weight, so I converted from high-test Pepsi to Diet. I didn't address the fact that I was *drinking too much*; I switched because I could still drink the same volume without having to worry about the extra (1000+) calories each day.

Now, instead of calories, I'm worried about Nutrasweet. So, without another alternative, I've made an effort to cut back on the amount of soda I drink. We're talking baby steps, but it's a start.

The new Pepsi/itunes promotion hasn't helped much. One in three wins a free song! I now have a pocketful of winning caps, roughly 2 albums worth. I guess if you do the math, 20 winners at one in three, means that I drank roughly…let's not go there. Like I said earlier, baby steps.

One of the songs I plan to pick is Outkast's catchy (and overplayed) *Hey, Ya*. OK, pick up your jaw and take a deep breath. I know it's a little out of character, but there's a story here.

A little over a month ago, Nora struck an interest in a set of toy rattles. They're various shapes and colors, and come inside a ball with holes corresponding to the shapes. Eventually, she'll master that concept, but for now, the rattles provide plenty of entertainment for her.

Nora soon realized that shaking the toys made noise. Her method of choice is to palm one, raise her arm up over her head, and wave her clenched fist around like the Dog Pound on the now defunct Arsenio Hall Show. It's even cuter when she realizes you're watching her, and she really starts to ham it up, adding a giggle and some bouncing.

Kelly would often encourage her by singing *"shake it like a Polaroid picture!"* Now, before I admit that I'm no longer part of the cool crowd, and know what songs/groups are popular, you have to understand that Kelly often comes out with this type of goofy thing. She makes up lyrics to songs, and has more nick-names for Nora, Bailey, and myself than I can count. So when I heard *"shake it like a Polaroid picture!"* for the first time, I laughed and thought it was her quirky sense of humor.

I know now I was wrong. And to make matters worse, I actually bought that album as a Christmas present for a *future* family member. (The countdown is on Mike. Soon you will also be able to say that Pat is your favorite mother-in-law!)

So mostly out of a sense of nostalgia, one of my many winning caps will be redeemed to download an Outkast song.

You know, now that I think of it, Kelly also sings another funny line to Nora when she's dancing.

She's a brick, house...

Could that be...

April 05, 2004

Cherry Picker

I've been good lately. I've stayed away from the political arena. With more than seven months to Election Day, it already feels like the conventions are here. Both sides have taken off the gloves and come out swinging. I've tried to avoid the name-calling and finger pointing, and feel I've done a good job. However, a storm's been brewing and now it's on the horizon.

I've endured the countless complaints and never ending whining of John Kerry. Each night I hear him say that George Bush has done an awful job with this or that, and that the country is going to the dumps. With each empty criticism, Kerry pledges, "I will do better" or "You can count on me to turn things around." Yet, he has not stated how he may improve the state of the country. And if my instincts are correct, he never will.

There are a number of characteristics I think are essential in choosing a President. But far and above any, is that the candidate must be a principled and trustworthy person. I like to know that the person I vote for believes in what he/she is saying. I guess the best way to put it is that in order to connect with someone I need to feel they are genuine.

I get that feeling from George Bush. Yes, I voted for him. Yes, I will again. No, I do not agree with everything he says and does (i.e. environment, gun control). But, he has a set of principles, based mostly on his faith, which he uses as a guide in making policy and he is consistent in what he says because he acts in accordance with his beliefs.

Last week, Bush signed a bill expanding fetal legal rights. The law makes it a crime to harm a fetus during an assault on a pregnant woman. People on both sides of this issue have said the new law will have far-reaching consequences. Abortion opponents welcome it as a step toward greater protections for the unborn, while the pro-choice crowd says the measure represents the first recognition in law of an embryo or fetus as a separate person.

The signing of this bill by Bush was expected. He has made his stance known on the abortion issue. He knows the country does not believe in a complete ban of abortions, and has not pushed the country in that direction. Yet, he remains steadfast in opposition to abortions except in cases of rape or incest or when pregnancy endangers a woman's life. That position has become a standard line in most of his speeches. This bill is an example of staying true to principles.

John Kerry voted against the bill. I can respect that. The pro-choice side has its point of view, as does the pro-life side. This issue has polarized the voting public for decades, and it's foolish to think either side is entirely correct. The context in which Kerry voted against the bill is where I have a problem.

Kerry is Catholic.

According to his campaign website (www.johnkerry.com), Kerry was "raised in the Catholic faith and continues to be an active member of the Catholic Church." He made this apparent last month by speaking at a Mississippi church and quoting the Bible. At that appearance he criticized President Bush for not being a "compassionate conservative." The verse he chose was James 2: 14, "What good is it, my brothers, if a man claims to have faith but has no deeds?"

Kerry supports abortion.

Contradiction? At the least Kerry ought to be very careful whom and how he criticizes. Kerry claims to "have faith" by being Catholic, but "has no deeds" by opposing the protection of life. Make no mistake; there is little to no wiggle room for Kerry. The Catholic Church is *more than explicit* on its view on abortion. The following are taken directly from the Catechism of the Catholic Church (Part 3, Section 2, Article 5, 2270–2275):

> 2270 Human life must be respected and protected absolutely from the moment of conception. From the first moment of his existence, a human being must be recognized as having the rights of a person, among which is the inviolable right of every innocent being to life.

> 2271 Since the first century the Church has affirmed the moral evil of every procured abortion. This teaching has not changed and remains unchangeable. Direct abortion, that is to say, abortion willed either as an end or a means, is gravely contrary to the moral law.

> 2274 Since it must be treated from conception as a person, the embryo must be defended in its integrity, cared for, and healed, as far as possible, like any other human being. Prenatal diagnosis is morally licit, "if it respects the life and integrity of the embryo and the human fetus and is directed toward its safe guarding or healing as an individual. It is gravely opposed to the moral law when this is done with the thought of possibly inducing an abortion, depending upon the results: a diagnosis must not be the equivalent of a death sentence."

Is this kind of contradiction acceptable? I know one doesn't always have to agree with everything groups they belong to stand for, but this is a fundamental principle of the Catholic Church, based on the 5th Amendment and the Church has taken an unyielding stance on it.

I think this is going to dog the Kerry campaign through to November. In the end, it may not decide the election, but it's just one of many examples of how Kerry "manipulates" his role/beliefs to appeal to as many people as possible.

I think it's dangerous to cherry pick religion. It's nice for Kerry to say he's Catholic, to appeal to a portion of the religious right, but if he does so, he better walk the walk. You can't have the easy parts of religion without standing up for the difficult, controversial aspects.

That's what makes a genuine person appealing. They are willing to face the crowd when times are tough.

April 07, 2004

Taper Madness

Boston is 12 days away, and although that's less than two weeks, I'm already itching to toe the line!

Part of the preparation for racing a marathon includes a taper. It's the period of time (usually about two weeks) immediately prior to the race. Weekly mileage is cut rather substantially, and you allow your body to fully recover after months of hard work. Daily runs are quite easy, with a greater emphasis on shorter, quicker workouts. The purpose is to sharpen up for race day. As coaching legend Bill Bowerman told his prized thoroughbred Steve Prefontaine, "the hay is in the barn!" He meant that the work was done, and preparation was complete.

The most difficult part of this final two weeks is the wait! Race day can't come fast enough, and the lessening daily release of pent up physical energy is transferred into nerve-racking anxiety. In an attempt to deal with the overwhelming excitement, I talk incessantly about the trip; when we're leaving, what we'll eat, who will go to the Expo, how will I get to the start, etc.

Kelly and Nora will live, eat, and breathe Boston, by default, with me. Thank goodness for a supporting family that will put up with me over the next 12 days! Tonight, I start packing.

April 12, 2004

Awareness

> I learned this, at least, by my experiment: that if one advances confidently in the direction of his dreams, and endeavors to live the life which he has imagined, he will meet with a success unexpected in common hours.
>
> In proportion as he simplifies his life, the laws of the universe will appear less complex, and solitude will not be solitude, nor poverty poverty, nor weakness weakness. If you have built castles in the air, your work need not be lost; that is where they should be. Now put the foundations under them.

Henry David Thoreau

I've been running consistently for over three years now. When I started back in the summer of 2000, I had no intention of ever running a marathon. I mostly wanted to prove to myself that I could commit to a goal, get back in shape, and be competitive once again.

After six months, I worked through the rustiness, and that old *fire* I worried was gone forever, returned. I was racing, and happy to once again be able to call myself a *runner*.

Early fall of 2001, I saw an advertisement for the Vermont City Marathon. I was confident after a successful return to running, so I registered, and in May 2002, completed my first marathon. I would have loved to qualify for Boston in that race, but it wasn't until five months later at the Mohawk-Hudson Marathon that I hit the mark.

I've attempted four marathons since with varying degrees of success. At the 2003 Vermont City Marathon, I bettered my qualifying time, but followed it with two straight DNFs (did not finish).

I used the time I ran in Vermont as my Boston qualifying time, and registered in December. I took some time off, and committed to an intensified training schedule to prepare.

As I'm writing this, the 108th Boston Marathon is one week from today. I've done the work, and am ready to race, but unexpectedly, training for this race has changed my perspective on many things.

I have always run to race. Training was just a means to an end, something that I had to do, and never really enjoyed. Satisfaction came from racing. However, after a couple disappointing marathons, I realized that I spend hours and hours, week after week, month after month training for a three hour race. When all that you have invested is riding on a single point in time, you are setting yourself up for failure.

This past fall, I had run more mileage and was in better shape than I was for any of my other marathon attempts, but ended up dropping out on race day. Does that mean that the previous months of training were wasted?

I started to realize that goals themselves don't mean as much once they're reached. Once I qualified for Boston, the quest was over and I was looking for something else to accomplish. The reward was fleeting and I had already moved on.

Note: I don't mean to diminish the importance of having goals and dreams. They are often the impetus that drives us through the process. But the process is what is important and what should make us happy.

Benjamin Hoff (*The Tao of Pooh*) eloquently explains that if we add up all the rewards in our lives, we won't have much. But if we add up all the spaces between the rewards, there's quite a bit. He used the example of Winnie the Pooh eating honey, his favorite food. That moment just before Pooh put a paw full of honey into his mouth is when he became happy and knew it. Hoff called it *awareness.* If we can learn to enjoy the process, we can stretch that awareness out so that it's not just an instant in time.

I started today by quoting from Walden, by Henry David Thoreau. I chose the quote because it recognizes the importance of dreams, and actively engaging life in order to achieve those dreams. The quote even goes further by sharing a path by which this is possible. Make life simple. If your head's in the clouds, that's OK, that's exactly where it should be. Change the things in life that you can, to make things less complex.

The image Thoreau used of building a castle in the air is perfect. The castle is a dream, with nothing to support it. His advice is to build a foundation from below to meet the bottom of that castle. Do what is needed to fill in that gap between the ground and your dream. Simplify your life to the things that are necessary to accomplish what you set out to do. The more complex our lives are, the more directions we are pulled in, and our focus is spread. Stick to the things that are important, keep perspective, and tune out all the *noise* around you.

Which brings me back to Pooh. Building a foundation or enjoying the process, they're both saying the same thing. Appreciate the present. If you spend all your time hoping and working for something in the future, someday it will come and pass. Then what? Start over? That's kind of depressing.

So as my training is winding down to race day, it has hit me how enjoyable the last few months have been. I'm going to Boston, and I will run well. I'm strangely confident about that. But this time, the end result will not determine the importance of the last few months. I've learned to enjoy each run with the same vigor.

Boston will be fun, and I'll enjoy it more, now that the experience won't hinge on accomplishing a specific time. I'm looking forward to the mass start, the screaming wall of Wellesley women, the Newton Hills, Heartbreak, and the finishing stretch down Boylston Street.

And if my intuition is correct, the end result will reflect the relaxed, confident attitude I've recently acquired.

April 21, 2004

Baking in Boston

The marathon can humble you.

Bill Rodgers

I've delayed writing about my 2004 Boston Marathon experience for a couple days. I wasn't exactly sure how or what I wanted to focus on. It would have been easy to fixate on my finish time, which was well over an hour slower than my qualifying time. I did have a goal going into the race of running near the three-hour mark, but it just wasn't in the cards Monday. Mother Nature decided to throw the 20,000+ runners an extra challenge by unleashing an intense 7-hour heat wave just as the marathon was about to begin. The eighty-five degree heat certainly took its toll on me, and forced me to adjust my game plan several times throughout the day.

Now two days removed, I can say the weekend was a runner's dream. I rubbed shoulders with two past champions (Greta Waitz and Greg Meyer), ran the most storied marathon course in the world, and have memories that will last forever. Although the race itself was grueling to say the least, I wanted to share the good with the bad. So after much thought, I've decided to focus this post on the last 6 miles of the race.

What? You mean the part where you were walking 16-minute miles in the scorching sun hoping some drunken BC student would knock you over and put you out of your misery?

Yes.

After turning right onto Commonwealth Avenue at roughly 17 miles into the race, I had realized any hope of salvaging a respectable time was gone. I was drained physically and mentally, and was entering the famed Newton Hills, which culminate with Heartbreak Hill. The night before the race, Kelly and her family decided the best place to await my arrival would be near the 20-mile mark. It was only a mile from Keri's house, where we stayed for the weekend (Keri/Mike…Thanks again for everything!), and would be easy to get to without having to try to fight traffic. Seeing them was my next focus, which carried me to 20 miles.

A touch before I expected, I heard Kelly yell as I was directly even with her. I assumed they'd be on the left side of the road (the direction they came from), but they moved across the street to keep Nora out of the direct sunlight. I gave them a quick wave and kept on moving. In hindsight, I should have stopped to say Hi and rest a bit, as the wheels really fell off shortly thereafter.

Just a quarter mile further I noticed I was no longer sweating, and my singlet and shorts were bone dry. I had been drinking roughly 14 ounces of fluid (a combination of Gatorade and water) EVERY MILE up to this point. If my math is correct, that's over 8 liters of fluid, and I was still dangerously dehydrated.

I struggled up Heartbreak, and took my first walk break. I walked for roughly five minutes, and attempted to *run* again. Not more than 10 steps later, my heart rate began to race, and my breathing became labored. I certainly wasn't moving fast enough to be winded, and I knew pushing myself any further would be dangerous. So I once again began to walk.

The marathon is a funny event. I've said in the past that anyone can run 20 miles, and I truly believe it. But to complete a marathon, it's different. That last 10K is critical. Physiologically, the human body can store enough glycogen to fuel a runner through about 20 evenly paced miles. After that point, you're body becomes less efficient and running becomes much more difficult. Over the course of my short marathon career, I've learned that once you reach this point, the race is as much mental as it is physical. Your body is sending all kinds of signals saying it's tired, and wants to quit.

Those signals were loud and clear Monday. But, for a reason I can't honestly pinpoint at this time, I didn't quit. It could have been because I wanted the finisher's medal, or the honor of completing the Boston Marathon, or simply because I had no other way of getting home. But I think it was more than that. I wasn't running for time, or position, yet some competitive streak in me kept me moving.

Physically, it was just a matter of putting one foot in front of the other. Mentally, it was much more difficult. I tried every kind of game imaginable. At 22, I pictured the last 4 miles of my easy 8-mile training loop. At 23, I thought of walking the neighborhood 3-mile out-and-back with Kelly, Nora, and Bailey. At 24, I thought back to the day Nora was born, and how Kelly endured a day and a half of drug induced contractions.

Logically, it all made sense. Practically, none of it worked.

In the end, the last mile and a half, I made an effort to look at each runner that passed me. I figured that Dan Courneene, a friend from Plattsburgh, would have run me down by now, but I hadn't seen him. I thought that maybe a familiar face might give me a boost. I didn't know at the time he had already gone by, probably around 23 miles or so.

After a couple turns in downtown Boston, I hit Boylston Street. It wasn't the way I dreamed it would be, but I had enough of a spark to trot in across the line.

Now I know exactly what Bill Rodgers meant in the quote above. I was more prepared for this race than any other race I've run. I had trained more, worked harder, maintained focus, and stayed healthy. Yet, something came from left field, which I was not prepared for. To run a great marathon, so many factors need to come together. I guess that's what makes guys like Bill Rodgers so special. They did it time and time again.

So, will I get back up on that horse?

Ask me tomorrow.

April 27, 2004

Run For The Roses

The first weekend of May is fast approaching, and that means one thing. The Kentucky Derby!

The grandest event in horse racing will mark its 130th running this Saturday. I likely will forgo the traditional Mint Julep for a Molson, while I park myself on the couch for two of the most exciting minutes in sport. My brother, father and I have watched, wagered, and enjoyed the Derby faithfully for over 10 years now. Typically, I'd have an idea of whom the front-runners are and which horses to avoid. This year I'd have difficulty naming more than a handful of the entrants. I have to admit I'm woefully unprepared.

My interest in horse racing was sparked at a young age. A few times a year, when my brother and I were toddlers, my parents would plan a night out in Montreal with friends. They'd leave early afternoon and head to their favorite Chinese Restaurant, Ruby Foo's on boulevard Decarie. Located directly across the street was l'Hippodrome Blue Bonnets.

Contrary to what a toddler might picture running at a **Hippo**drome, Blue Bonnets was Montreal's harness racing track. The racetrack was hardly glamorous. Crowds were large, lines were long, and the air was so filled with smoke it looked like the inside of a sauna. My parents weren't, and still aren't, big gamblers, but they'd take a shot or two on each race. It was an enjoyable evening with friends, and hey, you had a chance to go home with more money in your pocket than you came with! That didn't happen often, and by the end of the night, a stack of losing tickets usually filled my parent's pockets.

The babysitters we had for those nights were high school kids of my parent's friends. We'd spend the night watching TV, eating junk food and soda, and continually coaxing them into letting us stay up "just a half hour longer!" Eventually we'd end up getting tired and fall asleep on our blanket to Hockey Night in Canada or Star Trek. The next thing we'd remember is waking up in the morning.

That morning, without fail, there would be a neat little stack of tickets on the floor in front of both our beds. We'd jump up and look at the numbers corresponding to the horses, races and wager amount. Some of the tickets were flat in their original crispness, and others were wrinkled, likely the result of coming out on the wrong end of a photo finish. Nonetheless, they were all interesting to us. Those losing tickets could not have been a better *souvenir*. (BTW…Those tickets contained the first French words in my vocabulary: cheval, course, gagnant, place, classe, conducteur, cote, depart, bourse)

Once we were old enough, we went to Ruby Foo's and Blue Bonnets as a family. As a parent myself, I can appreciate my Mom's reluctance to release her hawk-like grasp on our arms while at the race track, as seedy looking characters were the norm. But for us, there were horses, huge hotdogs and greasy french fries, all kinds of action, and we were up late!

We couldn't place bets, but we'd pick the horses and my Dad would get the tickets. Our method of picking was usually related in some way to the horse's name or color. I was especially partial to the grey horses and horses with "hats." We'd hit a winner every now and then, including one longshot at 17–1. I quickly learned that those odds put $34 in my pocket!

Since then, Blue Bonnets nearly went bankrupt, was sold, and is now l'Hippodrome de Montreal. The environment is completely different. The track is bigger, betting has been simplified with the use of autotote machines, and best yet, 90% of the facility is smoke free. The hotdogs and french fries may still take a year off your life, but I'm in line as soon as I set foot in the clubhouse.

Like the facility, we too have changed. At some point this week, either Spencer or I will download a list of the Kentucky Derby entries and their past performances. We'll study those previous races and look for some pattern. We'll factor in breeding, Beyer ratings, and even the weather. *"Hey look, this one's a mudder!"* Instead of just picking a winner, we'll likely bet exacta boxes and triple keys. Spencer has had a fair amount of success in this manner. He regularly ends the day with more money than he starts with. But, as the whole pari-mutuel betting system requires, there are more losers than winners. And in terms of my horse-picking prowess, my money is going right into my brother's pocket!

So with the idea of simplifying my choices, I've decided to go back to what works. I took a quick peek at the entries in this year's race and have made my choices. I'll be betting on *Wimbledon* and *Imperialism*. Don't bother looking them up on any chart or handicapping publication. Just watch the post parade minutes before the start. They'll stand out, as they're the only grey horses in the race.

May 11, 2004

Spill

Parenting is tough.

Nora took her first spill yesterday at daycare. It wasn't a disaster, but she did get a pretty good smack on the forehead. She was trying to stand, using a small bench as leverage, but tipped and fell head first into a strip of electrical conduit on the wall. She cried for a little while, refused any ice or cold compress, and was back playing within 15 minutes. That's my girl!

Nora's teacher called the Pharmacy shortly after it happened, and Kelly quickly drove cross-town to see Nora. She had a two-inch black and blue streak across her forehead and an egg like you'd see on Wile E. Coyote when the Road Runner drops a boulder on his head. Although Nora seemed unfazed by the whole event, Kelly decided to take the rest of the day off and bring her home.

I know this is probably just the first of many bumps and bruises she'll experience, and maybe I'll be hardened by repetition, but it was difficult sitting at my desk at work knowing she was hurt. Part of me thinks that had I been there, it wouldn't have happened. But, that's not only unrealistic; it's kind of arrogant. She's already growing up, and pushing the envelope. With each second she takes her hand off my leg and stands on her own, you can see the confidence building in her eyes. As much as I'd always like to be there to catch her when she falls, I know she's learning by leaps and bounds.

Before bed last night I ran my hand across her bruise. She looked up at me and smiled the same way she does whenever I tickle her face or play with her hair. The morning fall was the farthest thing from her mind, a learning experience stored for future use.

For Dad, though, that learning experience was tougher to handle…one that will take a little longer to recover from.

May 14, 2004

Burpee's

This past Saturday I ran the 4.4-mile Charlie Pratt Memorial Route 9 Road Race. The race has been run for well over 20 years, and has become an annual tradition for me.

The event was first organized as the Burpee's Road Race in the early '80s. It started at a genuine, small town five-and-dime in Lewis, NY, across from a beautiful white Catholic Church. The point-to-point course followed Route 9 to the Social Center in Elizabethtown, NY. The first ¼ mile is uphill, with the remaining 4 miles gradually down to E'Town. It's a great course to really let the legs roll.

I don't remember if we attended the first, or second, running of the race. At the time, my Dad was the only serious, competitive runner in the family. I was in 5th (maybe 6th) grade. Although each year the race drew many of the top runners in the area, it was billed mostly as a family event. The fondest memories I have are of a huge buffet lunch, endless amounts of canned soda, and an award for being the youngest finisher.

Race morning we'd drive south on the highway to exit 32. Registration was always at the finish line (seems kind of backwards), but it gave us an opportunity to drive the course to scope things out. My dad always believed it was a good idea to preview the course, so "you knew what was coming".

I don't remember many details about the race itself. I just know that 4.4 miles seemed more like a marathon. After the race we ate, recovered and talked. One of the signatures of this event is that each year the results are put on large poster boards and preserved. These poster boards are then displayed at the next year's race. It's interesting to see how you stack up against your old times!

As the boards show, I raced consistently through the '80s and just into the '90s. This corresponded to the time I was in either high school or college. I then "retired" from racing for quite some time…nearly eight years. I reappeared again in 2001, and have not missed since.

The night before this year's race I decided to place extra emphasis on carboloading, or in other words…*beer and pizza!* Keith, a retired (soon to be un-retired?) runner and friend, and I grabbed a Zachary's veggie pizza for dinner. This was a major shift from the standard half-pepperoni/half-onion pizza that Kelly and I typically split. I have to admit my sense of adventure paid off…it was delicious! I even ate the olives…*did you hear that, Kelly?…I even ate the olives!* We then spent the remainder of the night shooting pool at Meron's.

Note: Like the Burpee's Race, Meron's is woven into the fabric of our family history. My parent's met there while my Mom was in college. My Dad would sit at the bar with, among other friends, Kelly's uncles, and my Mom would show up with her sorority sisters for beer and one of Meron's renowned burgers.

Race morning I woke up and traveled that familiar stretch of highway to exit 32 and into Lewis. And although I've run the course close to 15 times, I once again drove the course from start to finish, being sure to carefully watch my odometer to confirm the mile markers were accurate.

Once the race started, I quickly realized it wasn't going to be my day. This was made even clearer when a father my age darted out in front of me pushing a three-seat baby stroller...*filled with kids!* There's a difference between an off day and shear embarrassment...and, you can call it pride if you'd like, but I wasn't going to let that damn stroller beat me up that hill!

As awful as I felt, I worked my way up to, and past, all four of them, and started to feel pretty good about myself. That is, until I hit the mile mark.

The young woman standing there called out...*5:22, 5:23, 5:24...!*

Not good! A 5:24 first mile, uphill, on a day I knew I didn't have it in my legs. Look out...here comes the pain train! Or wait, it's not a train...*it's a baby stroller!*

I heard the wheels approaching, and a little voice yell out, *"Pass him Daddy, when are you going to pass him, Daddy?"*

Out of oxygen, tired, and short on patience, I wanted to reach out and grab that little...

It's a family race. ***Art, it's a family race!***

Mile 2 was 5:48, still respectable and still holding off Super Dad and crew.

About a half mile later, I slowed to grab a couple cups of water, and off they went...not to be seen again until the finish, when those kids were enjoying a huge buffet lunch and an endless cooler full of canned soda.

I imagine if those kids are brought up similar to the way we were, they'll soon be running for a chance at the youngest finisher award.

That's fine with me...I remember how proud I was getting that trophy. And, it'll save me the embarrassment next year of getting beat by their Dad and his magic bus.

May 23, 2004

Pink Eyes For A Straight Guy

It's been a busy week.

We've dealt with conjunctivitis, fever, horrible headaches, an ear infection and a raspy, hacking cough. All three of us have had some combination of these symptoms. Nora, we believe, started the whole deal, but thankfully seems affected the least. Probably due to the early impact of Augmentin, which neither Kelly or I were privy to. Whatever mutant bug caused this, it really kicked us in the proverbial tushy.

Along the way we made visits to the Pediatrician, Fast Track, and Hannaford (we do have to eat). Probably the most amazing of all was that Kelly managed to host a bridal shower for her sister, and as long as nobody calls in the next few days for the name of the eye drops I'm using, I'd say it went superb.

I missed three days of work and…hold your breath…SIX days of running! I haven't missed that many consecutive days since 2000 (including my near death experience in Boston).

The missed runs couldn't have come at a worse time. I'm running the Vermont City Marathon next Sunday, and was hoping to get one more week of sharpening in before the race. I had originally planned to race just the first half of the marathon for a PR, but I'm afraid this past week may have taken a bit of the zip out of my legs. So now, I hate to admit, I'm thinking of doing the whole thing.

A friend, and training partner, from Peru is hoping to run near 3:15, which is the time I now need to re-qualify for Boston. When I see her out on the roads tomorrow morning, I may ask her if she'd like some company on race day. Having someone to run with, I hope, will keep those awful memories of Boston in the back of my head.

But, above all, I'll be watching the weather. If I start to see numbers beginning with a 7 or 8, I'll be making the trip to Vermont only to pick up my T-Shirt.

This old dog may be dumb enough to hop in another marathon, but he won't get *burned again.*

June 01, 2004

Vermont City Marathon

My marathon woes continue.

Sunday I ran the Vermont City Marathon. The result…a DNF (did not finish) at 16 miles.

Since Boston, I continued to flip flop on whether I wanted to run the whole distance at VCM. At times I thought I'd just run the first half in an attempt at a half marathon PR. However, that idea was dismissed when I came down with a nasty cough/cold/sore throat two weeks ago, which I just could not shake.

I made the final decision to attempt the full distance on Tuesday, five days before race day. I ran eight on Wednesday and took the remainder of the week off, to allow myself to fully recover. It didn't happen. That nagging cough stuck with me, and ultimately led to my DNF.

Race morning my Dad and I drove to Burlington and reached the starting area about 30 minutes before the start. I was feeling quite good. My legs were rested and, dare I say, I felt *healthy*. My goal was to start slow, and work into a 7:00 pace.

Ambitious? Yes. But, this was my eighth marathon start. I've finished five, and no longer feel the need to prove I can finish. If I'm going to start, I'm going to run for a personal best. The details (if anyone is interested):

1–7:52 Started further back in the pack than normal…or in other words, my way of forcing myself to go out slower.

2–6:53 Good.

3–6:56 Nice and consistent. Finding my groove.

4–6:42 This mile is always a touch fast, as it contains a good downhill. Last year I ran it in 6:09, so I was happy to see that I maintained control this time around.

5–7:09

6–7:01

7–7:04

8–7:23

9–7:19

10–7:02 My legs felt great. Just over 7 minute pace, and well below personal best pace (3:08). Unfortunately, I'd been coughing constantly throughout the first ten miles. Not just a little throat tickle kind of cough either…more like a hack-half-your-lung-up kind of cough. My stomach muscles felt like they were doing the running.

11–7:23

12–7:23

13–7:38

Half–1:34:36 This was quite encouraging. As bad as the two weeks before were, and as bad as the hacking cough was, I was still on sub 3:10 pace…near a PR, and well under Boston Qualifying time of 3:15. But things only go downhill from here.

14–7:46

15–8:20 This mile includes Battery Hill.

And that's it. I didn't make it to 16. I calculated my likely finish time, factoring in my sinking pace/mile, and figured I had no chance at qualifying. Then it was just a decision whether to finish or not. I would have liked to carry on, but given that my body had taken quite a beating over the past 15 days, I decided to call it a day.

So where does this leave me now? I'm definitely in a "marathon rut". My first four marathons were 3:15, 3:10, 3:16, and 3:08. I've now followed those with a DNF, DNF, 4:18, and DNF. I think it's safe to say that's a trend.

I may just need a break from the distance. This summer I'll focus on shorter, quicker stuff…maybe work on my confidence. I'll be running the Bug Run 5K in Saranac Lake on June 12th and the Standard Life 10K in Montreal on the 19th.

If I decide I want to tackle Boston again next year, I'll have a chance to run a BQ time late this fall. But for now, I'm going to put thoughts of the marathon in the back of my head. My day will come…there's no need to rush it.

June 07, 2004

Thanks, Mr. President

"Whatever else history may say about me when I'm gone, I hope it will record that I appealed to your best hopes, not your worst fears; to your confidence rather than your doubts. My dream is that you will travel the road ahead with liberty's lamp guiding your steps and opportunity's arm steadying your way."

Ronald Reagan—1992 Republican Convention

I spent much of this past weekend tuned into C-Span, taking the opportunity to catch as many of President Reagan's speeches as possible. I was a 10-year-old kid when Reagan was elected to his first term. I was more interested in street hockey, swimming, and likely, getting my teeth drilled, than politics. But something about Reagan caught my interest.

I started listening to his speeches, and slowly became more interested in issues.

I remember the day he was shot.

I remember the re-election campaign, and how happy I was when Mondale only won his home state of Minnesota and the District of Columbia…which I discounted as "not a real state anyway."

I remember the President in West Berlin, emphatically demanding, "Mr. Gorbachev, tear down this wall!" To this day, those are the most spine-tingling words I've heard a world leader utter.

I remember his farewell speech, after serving as President for eight years, and how he described to us how he saw America as a "shining city upon a hill."

I remember the 1992 Republican Convention, from which I took the quote above.

And I remember the announcement he made disclosing his affliction with Alzheimer's disease.

But the one thing I most remember, and admire, about Ronald Reagan was his undying devotion and love for his wife, Nancy. Side by side they traveled life together.

Ronald Reagan's outlook and optimism helped shape my view on the world. Over the past few days, I've been struggling to come up with a fitting tribute…I've even considered traveling to Washington to pay respects in person. I have a few days to decide…but for now, I'll continue to listen to the speeches, and re-live the enthusiasm he created every time he spoke.

Thanks, Gip.

June 14, 2004

Reflection

I decided mid-week that traveling to Washington to honor President Reagan was not practical. Kelly was working Thursday night, and I also wasn't too keen on spending my first night away from Nora. I chose instead to take a half-day on Friday to watch the funeral at home.

I watched and listened to Margaret Thatcher, Brian Mulroney, George H.W. Bush, and George W. Bush eulogize the former President. All spoke with an intimacy not commonly seen at formal, state funerals.

Irish Tenor Ronan Tynan sang the most stirring version of Amazing Grace I've ever heard. The strength of his voice in the majesty of the National Cathedral sent chills down my spine. [On a side note…if you ever need inspiration, read a little on the life of Ronan Tynan. He had both legs amputated below the knee following a motorcycle accident when he was in his 20s. He followed that by winning 18 Paralympic gold medals, including world records in the shot put, discus, and long jump. As if that wasn't enough, he became a medical doctor and now one of the most accomplished vocalists in the world.]

And I felt the pride of being American at every formal military protocol on display. The crisp movements, 21-gun salutes, the horse drawn caisson, and the incredible detail and reverence for the handling of the flag were all a testament to the honor of President Reagan.

When the sun went down in California, and there was no more to watch, I started to reflect on how well people knew President Reagan. Each eulogy, each interview, while personalized, touched on all the same points. Reagan stood for freedom. He loved to laugh. He was a very religious man. And above all, he loved Nancy.

In a nutshell, that was the man. I knew that, sitting in my living room in Peru, NY. I felt like I had known him…that I had lost a friend. How did he do it? How did he make it so easy for all of us to know him so intimately?

I started to wonder how well people know me. What would people say at my eulogy? What kind of job have I done in letting people know who I am? Sounds simple, but is it?

Do people know that I, too, like jelly beans, but not nearly as much as I like M&Ms?

Do people know that I want to retire young…not because I'm lazy, but because there are so many things I want to experience?

Do people know that nothing is more important to me than my family?

Do people know I actually enjoy running marathons? (Up to 20 miles anyway)

Do people know I like to argue politics not because its fun, but because in my heart I feel what I say is true?

Do people know that the hour before Nora's birth was the most terrifying hour of my life? And the next hour was the happiest and most fulfilling?

And do people know that even though I'm a scientist by trade, I'm still a philosopher at heart?

I guess that's what funerals do...they bring on self-reflection. President Reagan touched the lives of all those around him, and in doing so, he changed the world. My goals aren't nearly as lofty. I'd settle for touching a few lives, and changing my little portion of the world.

June 23, 2004

I May Be Losing It

I'm thinking about getting a bike.

Somehow in the past few weeks I've been stung by the triathlon bug. This happened to me once before, two summers ago, but I successfully beat back the urge. I convinced myself it was a fruitless interest because I'm not a cyclist. I'm actually kind of afraid to get moving too fast on such a tiny piece of metal.

But there must have been a reason my interest was piqued then, and is again now. I swam as a youngster for the Northern Pikes, a competitive team based in Clintonville, NY. Granted that was a long time ago, but I think the swim portion will come back to me quickly. The running portion of the race will be my strength and will be what I'll rely on to keep competitive.

The bike leg has always been the wild card. I have no idea what to expect. I haven't actually been on a bike in years…5 or 6 years. And to be completely honest, I've never enjoyed riding a bike leisurely. It hurts my ass, and its difficult to talk to the person you're riding with.

So why a bike? Why the triathlon? My ass is still going to hurt, right?

The Lake Placid Ironman.

It's on TV. It's in the papers. I see people training. And I know people who have completed it. Yes, the whole thing…all 140+ miles…and multiple times at that!

And I have to say it impresses the hell out of me.

There really is no reason for me to want to compete in an Ironman. It's brutal. It's an entire day of pushing your body…and mind…to the limit. It has to be uncomfortable. What's the draw?

Maybe I have to *experience it* to understand why I want to do it.

Hey, at one point in my life I couldn't understand why people would want to run marathons.

I've now run 5.

June 28, 2004

Spackle Crap

OK…I admit this post will likely get me into a whole heap off hot water. It's probably not the kind of thing that the immeasurably proud parents of a nearly 11-month-old girl typically share. And further, it's not the kind of thing that anyone likely wants to read about. But…I just can't resist.

Once Nora began eating solid food, other things started becoming…uh…more solid too. In some ways this was a blessing. The frequency of leaks decreased exponentially, along with the Hannaford bags sent home from daycare with stained clothes and a nasty aroma. There's also typically no need for me to kneel down and say my "no explosive poopie prayer" prior to Nora's morning changing.

But with the good, comes the bad. The term *spackle crap* (copyright pending) was coined a few months ago, when with bated breath, I loosened the Velcro on Nora's Pamper. Instead of the typical watery, uncontrollable mess, I found a perfectly smooth wall of mostly digested carrots. At first I thought this was fantastic. A quick swipe with the Pamper and one baby wipe should get the job done!

Nope.

True to the best spackle job out there, every crease and crevice was filled to perfection. Those chunky little legs that everyone loves so much…yup…all three rolls filled to the gills. That first clean up must have been at least a 7 or 8 baby wipe job. There were so many used wipes inside the dirty Pamper, I couldn't stretch the Velcro enough to hold the thing closed!

Since then, I've perfected the wipe and fold, wipe and fold, wipe and fold. Now even the most powerful spackle crap can be handled with just 2 wipes! This unprecedented improvement is what earned me the title of Champion Diaper Changer.

I know this title won't be easy to hold. I'm sure Nora has more in store for me.

I've heard there's something called a *mega-volume poopie*.

Now that sounds like a challenge.

July 02, 2004

He'll Be Hail Marying All Night!

Last April I wrote one of the purposely few political entries you'll see here. I had gotten a little frustrated with the political banter, and even more frustrated with the acceptance of John Kerry's political views by the Catholic Church and its members.

He wants the benefit of being a part of the group, without having to actually believe in some of its most basic tenets. It's kind of like wanting to join the KKK because they have a sound economic policy, while trying to pull off not being a racist.

Apparently, others are frustrated as well. Kerry is being charged with heresy by a Catholic lawyer.

For the record…I think it's kind of kooky to go to this extreme.

But, I also think it's kooky that people don't see the hypocrisy in Kerry's actions.

July 07, 2004

Cycling Update

Two weeks ago I decided to give cycling a shot.

Kelly's brother, Jon, was nice enough to set me up with a nicer bike than I would have been able to buy. It was a perfect chance to try it out before committing to an expensive purchase.

I picked up the bike on a Sunday, pumped up the tires, dug an old helmet out of the basement and was ready to go. But, I didn't. I went for a run instead.

I put the ride off again on Monday, and Tuesday.

Every Wednesday night, a time trial is held at Point Au Roche. It's a low-key event, with roughly 20 people riding. The course is an out and back, 10 miles total, with only one real hill just before the turnaround (and even that isn't really a hill).

It would have been nice to at least sit on the bike before I raced for the first time, but that's me...jump right in before I even know how the gears work.

For those of you who know me...I'm mechanically challenged...and removing the front wheel to fit the bike in my Civic and returning it before the ride, is about the extent of my ability. (God forbid I get a flat and have to change a tube!) Therefore, it was imperative to arrive early to avoid the embarrassment of me wrestling with that damn tire!

I managed to get my bike set, and in my running shorts and baggy t-shirt, I signed up and was told I'd be fourth to go. Just prior to the first rider starting, I hopped on the bike and was thrilled to realize I had not forgotten what to do.

So there I was...on a bike for the first time in years...about to start my first race. I found a gear that felt OK, and before I knew it I heard:

"Art, 15 seconds..."

"Art, 5, 4, 3, 2, 1..."

I was off. And not a bad start, I might add. I started at a decent cadence, and as I picked up speed, I continued to shift into harder gears. Not even a mile into the race, I was in my highest gear, cruising along thinking this sport is a piece of cake...then my first mistake.

I can say now that I was in my highest gear...at that point in the race I didn't realize that. [Note: For all you cyclists out there, please forgive the awkward lingo and obvious ignorance.] I had moved through the gears so quickly that I assumed I still had more. I took a quick look down and honestly didn't know what the heck I was looking at. Is that big gear in the front easier or harder? I guess we'll find out. And I did it…I switched gears thinking I likely had more, and nearly threw myself off the bike as I flailed my legs around like a circus clown. I quickly switched back and learned the big gear is tougher than the little gear.

The rest of the race was pretty uneventful. I tried to stay consistent…but my legs were screaming very early on, and I found that toward the end, the only way I could keep a steady rhythm was to continually down shift.

I ended up riding the 10 miles in 31:32. It could have been worse. I was really hoping to crack 30 minutes. I did learn a lot, and think I'll be better prepared next time.

Looking back at the race, I think I was trying to muscle it too much. I've since been told that my cadence should be up near 90 RPM. I was nowhere near that in the race…in fact I'd be lucky if I was hitting 60.

Since that day I have been out only one other time. I planned a 15-mile ride this past Sunday. As I started I felt great. The route I chose had quite a few hills, so it was good practice working the gears to get to the top without coming to a standstill. After eight miles, I still felt fantastic, as I cruised down a steep hill on the River Road.

I then had an unfortunate encounter with a honeybee. I was wearing an old running t-shirt with plenty of room to fly into. When all was said and done, the little bugger stung me four times on the chest and stomach.

[It is now important to point out that I am allergic to bees!]

I stopped and quickly checked out the spots where I was stung. Red and slightly swollen. Well…so far so good. I was only about 3 miles from my parents, and closer to 6 from home, so I decided to zip into Peru and keep an eye on things. By the time I got off the bike, the welts were bigger and redder, but I had no signs of any other reaction. When I was young, I remember things like shots of adrenalin, the ER, and anaphylactic shock. Despite those wonderful memories, I wasn't too worried…but I wasn't going to take any chances.

After 20 minutes and a couple Benadryl, the welts started to go down. An hour later there were just a few spots where I was stung.

All in all, I made out better than the honeybee, who was lying crumpled on the corner of the River Road and Davern Road.

So…two rides in two weeks, with one crash and burn, and one near death experience. Am I really sure I want to continue with this sport?

The next ride will be Sunday, following a return to my feet for the Mayor's Cup 5K.

Thank goodness!

July 13, 2004

Etiquette

There are certain things in life that are never taught, but most people know. Whether we come across these pieces of knowledge through experience or just a "sense" of what's right is another debate, but generally people learn on their own.

The "facility" I most commonly use at work is rather cramped. Once you open the door, there are three urinals on the left wall, followed by three stalls. This all fits in roughly 20 feet lengthwise, so as you can imagine, there's not a real comfortable distance between gentlemen doing their business. [Note: for the women out there who have not been privy to the inside of a men's room, the stalls are just as you picture them. For the urinals...think pig trough, with a 6-inch space between each.]

Not too much thought is typically required when using the rest room, but there are a few important rules. Each time I use that rest room, I pick either urinal #1 or #3, assuming no one else is present. The obvious reason is that if someone else enters, they can use either #1 or #3 and we won't be rubbing elbows! I'd never go right to #2 because it *requires* that someone else stand directly next to you if they come in after you. Granted, if #1 and #3 are in use, a third person would have to use #2 or risk soiling themselves. In that case, it's perfectly fine to use urinal #2.

Good...I hope that little lesson was clear.

Now today...after break and my 20 oz. Diet Pepsi, I stopped and parked myself in front of urinal #1.

Then, not more than 5 seconds later, it happened.

Someone...a clueless, nameless someone...opened the door, entered the rest room, and started to use urinal #2!

The horror!

Was there something wrong with #3?

Did I not notice gobs of toilet paper, cigarette butts, and various other floaties clogging the drain of #3?

Doesn't this guy know that he should be using #3?

There I was at #1 with Mr. Oblivious just inches away, with tons of free space available.

Oh the horror!

As scarring as those 30 seconds were, I managed to regroup and have a productive afternoon. And I'm going to take solace in the fact that I've worked here for nearly 9 years and this is the first time I've encountered such a frightening occurrence.

And it could have been worse.

He could have looked over at me and smiled.

July 19, 2004

Nora attended her first wedding this past weekend at the beautiful St. Agnes Church in Lake Placid. Her Aunt Keri and (now Uncle) Mike are officially Mr. and Mrs. Hotarek. Sounds good.

I'm sure it'll take some time for Keri to get used to a new name, as it will take Mike time to stop fiddling with the ring on his left hand. Or, if he's at all like me, the fiddling will never stop, and he'll incessantly spin and twist and move the ring over his knuckle. [Note: I'm obsessive-compulsive, and the continuous, over-whelming urge to manipulate the ring on my finger is in no way representative of married life.]

The entire weekend was wonderful…packed full with family, friends, a beautiful view, heartfelt toasts, and food. But, I'm getting ahead of myself.

This was Nora's first wedding.

She and I spent a lot of time together Friday and Saturday. Kelly was Keri's Matron of Honor, and had responsibilities Friday at the rehearsal and most of Saturday for preparations and the ceremony.

The times when Kelly was busy, we went for rides, took a walk, ate Oatios, played with Grandma and Grandpa, or, on the rare occasion, took a nap. We even looked at a few bikes at Placid Planet Bicycles, although she seemed far more interested in a bin full of water bottles.

The rehearsal dinner was held at the Boathouse Restaurant. It would be difficult to find a more beautiful spot for dinner in Lake Placid. As the name suggests, the restaurant is an old boathouse directly on Mirror Lake. The dining area featured large, picture windows overlooking the Lake and a wrap-around porch, which enabled guests to enjoy the fresh air if they chose.

The rehearsal dinner made quite an impression on Nora. It was the first social event she'd been to in which she could eat REAL food. And you should have seen her eyes when she saw the mound of cheese out on the porch! The next 45 minutes were spent shoveling enough cheese into my little girl to bind up Shaquille O'Neal…but she loved it, and to our relief, there were no *difficulties* the next day.

By the time dinner was served, Nora was beginning to get overtired. My parents had planned each night to leave a little early, with Nora, so she could keep her routine and get a full night's sleep. This also allowed Kelly and I the opportunity to enjoy a "later than normal" night. [Our parents spoil us…and I hope we thank them enough for all they do.]

After an hour or two at the party, during which I and a few of the girls from the shop (Vickie, Carol, and Brenda) held up our corner of the bar, Kelly and I said good-byes and went to pick up Nora.

We slept well Friday night, with the exception of Nora waking up briefly at 5:00am for a snack. Thankfully she played for only 20 minutes, fell back asleep, and slept in with us until nearly 7:30. Just what we needed to refresh ourselves for what likely would be a long Saturday for Nora.

Wedding morning I went out for a 6.5 mile run around Mirror Lake. It was only 8:00am when I started, and already very humid, so I can't say I was all that excited about putting on my suit. I made sure I was back in time to shower, eat breakfast, and drive Kelly to Keri's room across town to prepare for the ceremony.

By 10:30 it was Nora and I. She hadn't slept much during the day, so I decided to take a drive to Saranac Lake. The car seat has the magical ability to lull her to sleep, regardless of how hard she fights it. It was a perfect day for a ride, the sun bright, the sky filled with puffy white clouds, and just enough sprinkling of rain to allow for numerous rainbows springing from Lake Flower.

I returned to the hotel at around 12:00, fed Nora, and relaxed. After lunch, Nora had one of her many visits from her cousins Christopher and Keith. They were fantastic with her the entire weekend…helping to keep her entertained when she was sick of being stuck in a stroller, high chair, or car seat.

The ceremony started a little after 2:00. I managed to get Nora to fall asleep, just before, and snuck her into the church, still strapped into her portable car seat. I said my own little prayer that she'd sleep through the service, but I chose to sit in the back just in case.

The parents were announced first, followed by the bride's maids, and Kelly. Nora slept through the initial singing, Pachelbel's Canon, and a few other organ songs. But, just before Keri made her entrance, the organist must have kicked up the volume. The traditional wedding march not only geared up the guests for the bride, it also woke little Nora, who discovered she was somewhere she hadn't been before. She quickly voiced her displeasure as I swiftly whisked her out the opposite side of the church.

I have to confess that I heard only bits and pieces of the remainder of the ceremony. Nora, Christopher, Keith and I spent most of it in the narrow lobby eating Oatios and talking with the photographer. [I have not seen the pictures, but he seemed to have done a fantastic job. I believe his name was Shawn Holes. Check out his site…at some point Keri's pictures will be displayed. Also, I didn't realize it at the time, but he took a picture from the top of the stairs heading to the balcony, looking down at Christopher, Keith, and I all hunched around the stroller looking at Nora. It has the potential of being a great picture…I hope it turns out OK.]

Nora was great. She let out an occasional loud giggle, but never a scream or cry, even though she was confined for over an hour. Following the ceremony, Nora was more than excited to see Mommy, who quickly nursed our little food-processing factory before heading off for pictures. [How Kelly managed to discreetly nurse Nora in the car wearing a strapless wedding dress is beyond me.]

We had almost two hours before the reception, so we went back to the hotel and made a failed attempt at one final nap. We ate dinner, played again with Grandma, Grandpa, Christopher, and Keith, and before we knew it, it was 5:00.

The reception was held at the Lake Placid Club, with a spectacular view of the Adirondacks and Olympic Ski Jump Towers. Nora met a bazillion (her word) new friends, and enjoyed all the excitement of the party. Once the cocktail hour was over, and the guests were all seated, the traditional best man's toast was made. Mike's longtime friend spoke plainly and from the heart. His words were moving, and clearly reflected the friendship he and Mike have.

The food arrived shortly later, and Nora had decided she had enough of her baby seat. I fenced in an area between myself, Kelly, a large picture window and Kelly's cousin Katie. That little play area on the carpeted floor, along with a spoon, wedding program, bread, and numerous visitors, kept her busy for the next two hours. In that time, Mrs. Poissant, Mr. Poissant, and two bridesmaids also spoke. By now, Nora had picked up on the laughing and clapping, and although delayed, enjoyed partaking in the lighter moments.

Finally, Keri spoke to all the guests in a way that only Keri could pull off. A perfect mix of emotion and humor, thankfulness and love.

Nora went off to bed not long before Kelly and I. As is always said about weddings, it's hard to believe its over. We've heard about these plans for months and months…and now the day has come and gone.

Nora has experienced her first wedding. And I'm sure if she could tell you herself, she'd say she had a ball. That is her favorite word…"Ball".

July 26, 2004

Induction

One year ago yesterday I left work knowing I wouldn't return until Nora was born. Kelly was already 3 days over her adjusted due date, and if nature did not intervene, she was going to be induced early Monday morning.

It was a nervous weekend. Over the course of nine months, we waited, patiently. Nine full months. And the last weekend finally came.

It's amazing how patient we were for so long, and how quickly that patience dissolved that Saturday. We knew the day we'd go to the hospital…Monday at the latest…maybe even sooner! Yet our patience was gone.

After all the anticipation.

After all the appointments.

After all the bloodwork, and monitors, and poking and prodding.

After 9 long months.

We wanted to meet our daughter.

It didn't happen that weekend, and Monday we drove to the hospital to start the induction process. By 9:00am we were checked in and in the birthing suite. And yes, it is a suite. A huge room, walk in bath, pullout couch, TV, and phone. It felt comfortable.

We talked a little. We were both nervous. But our nervousness had shifted. The chance that Kelly would go into labor, unexpected in the middle of a thunderstorm, alone in Peru with no car and no working phone line was gone. That extra bit of anxiety that comes with the inability to prepare for a specific day and time was now relieved. We were at the hospital. We knew that Nora would be born Monday or Tuesday. The fear of what was ahead was still present, more so for Kelly, but that we had prepared for.

The Doctor arrived within a half hour and explained that we'd start with Cervidil, the least objectionable form of inducement. Kelly would be hooked up to the monitor every couple of hours, but other than that, we were free to walk around the hospital, and even take a walk outside, as long as we stayed on hospital property. Kelly was comfortable, and the experience was actually fun.

After several checks with no dilation, it became apparent the Cervidil was not helping. Morning turned to afternoon, afternoon turned to evening and the Doctor stopped in one last time to talk over our options.

I say options, but really there were none. We'd get a good night sleep and start with Pitocin first thing Tuesday morning. Once again we had to be patient. A few visitors stopped by, we watched a little TV, and slept well in anticipation of a big day.

Tuesday morning our nurse quickly set-up the Pitocin pump. The drug is introduced at a constant rate through an IV tube. The dose starts low, as the drug affects each woman differently. Every 30 minutes or so, the nurse would check the heart rate and contraction monitors, and with nearly every visit, she'd increase the rate at which the pump administered the drug.

Obviously Kelly didn't need a stupid machine to tell her that a contraction was occurring, but the contraction monitor (I don't know what it's really called) was helpful for me. I sat by the chart recorder and watched the repeating sine-like wave grow and recede, grow and recede. The numbers on the control panel would climb and drop correspondingly, and right on cue, Kelly would say that another contraction had started.

Over the course of the next 6 hours Kelly became progressively more uncomfortable. The contractions were getting more intense and the period of time between them was decreasing. Periodic checks of her cervix showed no dilation at all.

My parents, and Kelly's mom and sister arrived at around 1:30pm. Kelly was definitely not comfortable, but her pain was manageable, and the company helped distract her from the constant flurry of contractions. I hadn't eaten all day, and was on the verge of starving, but I didn't feel right leaving Kelly at this point. However, when our families arrived, they convinced me to go down to the café to grab a sandwich. That ended up being a huge mistake.

I left Kelly in relatively good condition, but on my return to the room, I found that all hell had broken loose. Kelly was groaning in obvious discomfort, and she managed to tell me she had just sent for the anesthesiologist. Kelly was more than strong, and determined to attempt to avoid any unnecessary drugs, but the constant barrage of increasingly intense contractions finally was more than she could tolerate.

The anesthesiologist arrived shortly and maneuvered Kelly into position...sitting up, back exposed, and slumped over a pillow. A thin tube would be inserted into the area near her spine in which local anesthetics could be administered. The first attempt at inserting the catheter was unsuccessful, as was the second; prompting the Doctor to tell Kelly she had "alligator skin".

The third, thankfully, resulted in almost immediate relief. Within 20 minutes, we were all relaxed and joking, and even Kelly enjoyed watching the monstrous contraction peaks rolling on the chart recorder.

The next 4 or 5 hours were pretty uneventful. We talked, and did what we could to pass time, but it was evident that the Pitocin wasn't working either. By this point we were both pretty drained, and were really hoping for things to progress.

On the next routine monitor check, the nurse said she had contacted the Doctor, as Kelly had received about all the Pitocin that was safe to give. At the same time, Kelly was starting to get chills, and asked for an extra blanket. Shortly after getting the blanket, the chills turned into full-blown shakes. We called the nurse, who took Kelly's temperature, and informed us that Kelly had a fever of 104F. Now things got serious really quick. The Doctor was already on his way, and upon his arrival, we decided that an emergency C-section would be performed in roughly one hour. The OR was being cleaned following a prior C-section.

Kelly was prepped, I gowned up, and before we knew it, we were headed into the OR. I sat on a stool next to Kelly's head, and talked with her for roughly 5 minutes while the Doctor began the procedure. Long before I expected it, he directed me to stand if I wanted to watch Nora "being born". I stood, and gazed in amazement as he put two fingers under each of Nora's arms and rather roughly yanked her into the world. She let out a quick little scream, which Kelly, despite a significant drop in her blood pressure, immediately reacted to. She asked me if Nora was OK…and I happily said she was perfect!

I kissed Kelly on the forehead and joined the pediatrician as she cleaned, weighed and performed the APGAR test on Nora. She passed with flying colors, and to all our surprise she weighed in at a whopping 7 pounds 13 ounces!

It was close to an hour and a half before Kelly had recovered from surgery, and Nora was put through all the required checks/tests/picks/goop in the eyes. After the last test, and a quick hello to all our family still at the hospital, I pushed our new daughter in her bassinette through the hallway to the recovery room, to introduce her to her Mom for the first time.

It was a perfect fit. Just after saying hello, Nora latched on for the first time, and ate like she was the world nursing champion. Kelly's last worry was gone. We had a beautiful, healthy, hungry little girl.

We couldn't have been happier.

August 03, 2004

"Hi!"

Nora's learned a new word, "Hi!" And she loves to use it.

Every person she sees, she'll blurt it out, sharp and confident, then smile…that irresistible smile she has that makes you want to pick her up and squeeze her.

Kelly took her to Hannaford yesterday afternoon to pick up our weekly groceries. Up and down the aisles, and through the checkout, Nora happily said "Hi" to everyone she saw.

It's fun to watch the expressions of the people as they pass. Their faces lighten at the sound of Nora's tiny voice. Most will say hi right back, and some, much to Kelly's chagrin, will stop to talk a little.

When it comes to grocery shopping, Kelly ranks with the best of them. She's polite, yet purposeful. She has her route mapped out, and is always on the move. On the rare occasion that I go with her, I typically have to chase her down the last aisle after only getting sandwich meat. [I think it's her way of getting past the cookie section without having to hear me say…"mmmm, those look good (hint, hint)."]

Despite her attempt each week to get in and out of the store in world record time, she is still cordial with people. I too, make an effort to acknowledge people when they pass. A quick nod, a hello, or good morning…nothing formal, just my way of saying, "yes, I see you."

I wonder if Nora's desire to say hi to everyone comes from watching us, or if she's just social by nature. She must have at least some of both her Grandmother's genes, which with even the slightest amounts would make her more social than both Kelly and I together! It's likely a combination of both. She sees us doing something that she can imitate, and she likes people, so she's learning and expressing herself at the same time.

Not everyone is as polite as our little Nora.

Jon and I went on a great bike ride Sunday. We left from his camp on Fern Lake and rode roughly 3 miles to the turnaround on the out-and-back portion of the Ironman course. This section is 7 miles in length, with minimal traffic and beautiful views. Round trip, including a bit of a cool-down totaled 22 miles in roughly 1:15.

On the way out, we encountered 5 or 6 cyclists heading the opposite direction. Both Jon and I gave quick waves, with no response. Judging from their effort level, they weren't world-class cyclists, intently focused on their ride. It seemed they simply weren't interested in being friendly. We laughed about it and Jon joked they must be part of an unhappy people tour.

It's probably not fair to make judgments based on a couple days' experiences, but in this case it appears these events are a microcosm of life. I'm proud of my little girl. She's beginning to be a little person, full of her own ideas and thoughts. She's friendly, curious, funny, and full of energy. She loves to cuddle when she's tired, and plays non-stop when she's awake.

She's chosen to be the type of person that says hello when people pass. And I'm sure, when she learns the words, "how are you" will be added as well.

And if she's at all like her grandmothers, she'll learn how many kids they have, what they do for a living, what their favorite color is, etc…

August 06, 2004

Holy Technology!

I participated in my third Point au Roche time trial Wednesday, the first with my new bike. The other two races were mediocre performances at best. I started out with a 31:32 for the 10 mile, flat, out and back course. Two weeks later I improved slightly, to 31:14, on a windy day.

This time, with a blue, flower clad rocket beneath me, I screamed to a 28:28 finish. [OK, I got carried away with the *screamed* part…but it was still a PR for me by nearly 3 minutes!]

Could the bike make that much difference? I know it made some…but I think *I* can take *some* credit too. Well…even that credit should probably go to Jon, for suggesting that I focus more on cadence than muscle, and Danny, for letting me borrow his shoes, which allowed me to get away from the 8th grade style toe clips I'd been using.

The one thing I did do was execute my plan. I managed to stay on the lower ring the entire 10 miles, and never felt that burning accumulation of lactic acid in my quads that I experienced the previous two trials. I didn't have my computer properly affixed to my bike, so at the turnaround I had no idea what pace I had maintained. I did notice that I had only been caught by the person who started immediately behind me, which was also an improvement.

I rode scared the remaining five miles, and wasn't caught by another rider. A small, but satisfying victory!

I have to admit I'm beginning to really enjoy this sport. I ordered a pair of shoes online, and hope they arrive late Friday or early Saturday so I can get a couple longer weekend rides in. Also, I've been relatively good about maintaining my running mileage. I'm still averaging roughly 30 miles a week…about 10 miles/week less than I'd like, but still respectable.

[Don't tell anyone, but the Y-Tri is scheduled for Saturday, August 14th, and I'm getting quite the itch to give it a shot. **The swim you ask?** *Yeah, I know, I haven't done that in probably 20 years! But, I imagine it'll come back pretty fast. It's not the type of thing you forget how to do…kind of like riding a bike.]*

August 16, 2004

Y-Tri

I can now call myself a triathlete.

Saturday I competed in the Y-Tri at Point au Roche State Park. And I finished. So I'm no longer an aspiring triathlete…I'm the real deal.

Of course, my goal is the Ironman next summer, and I'd have to do what I did Saturday at least *6 more times, in a row, on the same day*…but it's a start.

The race was made up of a 0.5 mile swim, 18 mile bike and 4 mile run. I couldn't have asked for a better day. Particularly, no south wind…which would have made the swim more interesting than it already was.

I was nervous going into the race. I hadn't been in the water in years. And by saying I hadn't been in the water, I'm not talking about lap swimming, or swim lessons. I mean I can't remember the last time I got wet other than by taking a shower or getting caught in the rain running. So needless to say, when I took a look at the buoys heading straight out from the shore, I wasn't impressed.

Then a fellow swimmer was kind enough to tell me that it is difficult to judge distance over water. At first I was slightly relieved, thinking that maybe it looked further than it was. But he was kind enough to clarify for me that it was *further* than it looked! Great!

Just prior to the start, all the competitors mingle in thigh deep water until the race director blows the starting whistle. I took the opportunity to slide to the side and dive in for my first few strokes. Success! I floated, and the couple strokes I took felt OK.

Then I heard the race director yell "30 seconds". I pulled my swim cap over my ears, double checked my goggles, and was set to go. The whistle blew and we were off!

There were four buoys marking the line we were to swim. Each appeared to be evenly spaced, so I assumed they were roughly 100 meters apart. Before I hit that first buoy I was exhausted! My arms felt like my legs at 20 miles in a marathon…and if I tried to continue freestyle for too long, I couldn't keep up my breathing. I found I could get 5–6 strokes in, breathing to my left each stroke, before I had to switch to breaststroke. That gave me the opportunity to catch my breath, and give my arms a bit of a break from the extra energy required to lift them fully out of the water. It also allowed me to eye the rowboat gently coasting beside us, which was meant to rescue anyone in need. As heavy as my arms felt so early in the swim, I wanted to make sure to keep that damn boat in sight!

I hit the turnaround in decent shape, and made the mistake of looking down into the murky dark below. For those of you who don't know...*I hate swimming in open water!* Who knows what was under there, but I was certain it was going to reach up, grab my tired butt, and gobble me up as a boney morning snack.

I think that fear, and (more likely) the fact that I saw several people behind me, encouraged me to pick up the pace a little. I tried to count out 10 freestyle strokes before I popped my head up gasping. I'd breaststroke until I recovered, and try 10 more strokes. The counting helped distract me, and before I knew it I could see bottom. Had I been able to judge the depth better, I'd have put my foot down at neck level...anything to stop swimming! But, as it turned out, I was just over knee deep when I pulled myself up.

And *wow*...Wobble city! One of the warning instructions at the start of the race was to be careful coming out of the water, until you get your "land legs" back. When he said it, I didn't understand what he was talking about, but I do now. If you want to experience what I felt like, follow these steps:

1.   Stand up

2.   Extend your arms out and spin around for 30 seconds.

3.   Stop and try to stand up straight!

Good luck. At least I had the benefit of water on all sides of me helping to hold me upright.

The transition went smoothly. I took it easy, not really trying to speed through it. Wet suit off. Dry my feet. Socks. Bike shoes. Jersey. Helmet. Drink. And take off! My guess is that it took a solid three minutes...but those watching me may have a better idea of the time I took.

The bike course uses the same stretch of road as the weekly time trial, so I was familiar with the route. Other than an unfortunate incident with my pedals, the bike leg was pretty uneventful. [I stopped just a half-mile into the bike to remove my computer probe, which was rubbing against my spokes. And, once again, I only unclipped one shoe. I fixed the probe, but as I started to get moving again, I leaned too far to the opposite side and...*Timber!* Flat on my side...with my bike on top of me...next to the little shack where you pay to park! The attendants, along with the car driving by, must have gotten quite a show!]

I stayed steady throughout the bike leg, and by the end, caught about 10 people. I noticed that I'm starting to feel much more comfortable on my tri-bars. I spent nearly the entire 18 miles on them, only sitting up when I passed someone or made sharper turns.

As I came into the park to finish the bike, I noticed my overall time was 1:21 and change. I think my transition from bike to run went a little quicker. My guess is around 2–3 minutes. Which for me is astounding! When I go out for training runs at home, it's not uncommon for me to spend 10 minutes lacing up my shoes. Yes, I'm anal, neurotic, obsessive, compulsive…blah, blah, blah. So a quick change of shoes was a small victory.

Once the shoes were laced, I took a last drink of Gatorade, grabbed my watch and started the run. This was the most encouraging part of the day!

I felt great! The one aspect I was most worried about in competing in triathlons was that I might be too tired after the first two legs to take advantage of my strength…the run. My fears were soothed Saturday. I felt strong; like I had just run a long warm-up prior to a race, and before I knew it I was within the last half mile of the race.

I finished strong, and ended with a total time of just over 1:46. I didn't see the official result, so I don't know my times for each leg. I did, however, time the run with my watch. And as much as I'd like to think I really blistered the run, I think the course was short of 4 miles. My run, excluding the transition, was 23:11. I did feel great…but I don't honestly think I could go out and run that pace fresh right now! I'll be curious to get the official results to see how my run time stacked up against the rest.

All in all, my first triathlon was a success. I had a blast the entire race, and can't wait to hop in another. I still have a lot of improving to do on the bike, and the swim, well; I'm sure SOME training would help a ton.

It was hard for me Saturday morning knowing that I was competing, but was not going to be competitive. But as the race went on, I found that participating could be enjoyable as well. That'll work for the first time, but now I have a frame of reference. I may not be competitive on an overall basis next time either, but at least I'll have my own performance to better.

August 19, 2004

The Chair Police

After lunch today, I returned to my desk amid a bustle. My co-workers quickly let me know I was in "hot water".

The chair police were after me.

The company I work for has been going through major changes. People are switching jobs and offices on a daily basis. [This isn't by choice…can we all say *needs of business*?]

In many ways it's amazing that any work is getting done by anyone other than the custodians. And when you need to talk to someone, it's a crapshoot whether or not they'll be where they were the day before.

Last week I lost my plush corner office. It was a perfect spot…off the beaten path…quiet, new, comfortable. I'd been there for two years. That's about 23 months longer than I expected, judging from where I sit in the general pecking order of corporate America.

I lost my office to join Cubicle-ville.

I'm not complaining. I still have a job…and a paycheck…so I'm happy.

Relatively.

As I said before, the chair police were after me.

When I moved my cardboard box full of belongings from Carpetland to Cubicle-ville, I found that my new desk had no chair. I did as much scrounging as I could and picked the first non-stained, squeakless chair I could fine.

At the time, I didn't realize what I was doing!

Apparently, I had picked an "office chair". Not just a chair, an "office chair". These chairs, I now know, are for "office people", which I no longer am. I'm a member of Cubicle-ville, which means I have to kick, bite, scream, scavenge, and pillage to gain rights to a place to plop my boney butt.

So, head down, and chastised, I reluctantly relinquished my adjustable, lumbar supporting, Easy Glide Executive Chair to the office move coordinator.

Once again I went hunting.

And I found a winner.

The chair I now have used to support the butt of a member of Carpetland. We all have to start somewhere. Now any time I need a little encouragement or incentive to work harder, I'll just look down, between my legs and dream of what could be.

Yes, the days of Carpetland are gone for now, but the sweetness of my time there will not be easily forgotten.

At least until 4:30, when I hit the parking lot, on my way to see Kelly and Nora.

August 30, 2004

Perseverance

Yesterday morning, as I was eating a chocolate Pop-Tart before driving to Platts-burgh to meet Jon for a ride, I set the VCR to tape the Men's Olympic Marathon.

The news and papers have been filled with details on the historic course, run from Marathon to Athens, and finishing in a marble stadium built for the first modern Olympics in 1896. Most of the big names in the sport were racing, including world record holder Paul Tergat, in an effort to claim an Olympic gold at the birthplace of the 26.2 mile race.

But with hills, heat, and inspiration only the Olympics can provide, the final result was beyond imaginable.

Jon and I decided to ride an out and back 40-mile route. We had a strong tail-wind on the way out, and we cruised along at speeds I don't typically see on my bike computer. Even so, I felt comfortable. In fact, at the turnaround (exactly 20 miles), we were at 58 minutes and change. My fastest 10-mile time trial was roughly 28:30, so that's twice the distance at nearly the same pace. Granted the wind helped, but I was very happy with the effort.

Then...we turned back, and I realized why we had cruised so comfortably. The next 20 miles we were besieged with a constant wall of wind. No breaks, no breather. That ride now counts as the hardest effort I've had on the bike (including the triathlon and time trials). I even had the benefit of tucking in behind Jon the majority of the way back, and I still had everything I could do to stay on his tire.

Periodically during that last half of the ride I thought of the Olympic marathoners, who had already begun their race. It wouldn't be long before they hit the grueling, almost cruel, hills at 12 miles. Those hills carry the runners to 20 miles. The marathon course is widely held as the toughest Olympic Marathon course in history, and the hills would likely have a major say in determining the medalists.

So as the marathoners worked the hills, I dealt with the wind. And after arriving back in Plattsburgh, I felt good about my effort for the day. It was by far my best day on the bike, and now I could go home and wait for the marathon to end, so I could rewind the tape and watch the race in it's entirety.

The first 10 miles were pretty uneventful, with a pack of as many as 30 runners leading the way. Then true to my initial prediction that the hills would determine the race winners, Vanderlei de Lima (Brazil) made a bold and aggressive move shortly past halfway. Only a handful of the lead pack reacted, and with 10K remaining, three runners had separated themselves from the rest.

Then the unimaginable happened.

A drunken, defrocked Irish priest with a history of disrupting major sporting events flew across the road, grabbed de Lima, and drove him into the crowd of people lining the course.

A jackass from Ireland tackled the leader of the Olympic Marathon!

For those of you who have not run a marathon, I can say from experience that once you hit 20 miles any disruption in your running rhythm can result in disaster. Heck, I've had a hard time getting back in the groove when I slow too much at a water station. This guy was clinging to a 30 second lead, and had to peel himself off the pavement and somehow regain his composure. Thankfully, de Lima popped up almost immediately and continued on. But you could see on his face he was visibly shaken.

Suddenly, I was not only routing for the American, Meb Keflezighi, who was running in second. I wanted de Lima to hang on, pull things together, and maintain his hold on a medal. I was happy when I saw him post a 4:55 mile somewhere around 23.

An Italian, Baldini, and Keflezighi, caught de Lima shortly after the incident, and entered the stadium 1–2. Lima stayed tough mentally and held on for the bronze medal. As he entered the stadium he had a grin that lit up Athens. He extended his arms like wings and swayed back and forth across the lanes of the track.

At that moment, he provided the world a glimpse of the Olympic spirit. He had every right to be angry. He had every right to feel cheated. An unimpeded chance at a gold medal was taken from him by a freak in a skirt. Yet he was celebrating like a kid on Christmas. At possibly the lowest point in Olympic Marathon history, Lima's strength of will prevailed, and he crossed the line an Olympic hero.

Before yesterday at 1:30, I had never heard of the Brazilian named Vanderlei de Lima.

Then he attacked the hills of Greece alone.

He endured an unprecedented disruption 20 miles into the race.

He entered the stadium with surprising enthusiasm.

And finished with the grace of a true champion.

Thanks, Vanderlei de Lima, for showing the world how to deal with adversity. Thanks for staying the course, and giving us a model of courage in action. Your medal may be bronze, but you've provided us a golden memory.

September 13, 2004

Prince Edward Island

Today I returned to reality.

Kelly, Nora and I spent the past week in Prince Edward Island, Canada…sheltered from the world.

P.E.I. is roughly 750 miles northeast of Peru, and there is no real direct route there. Before the trip we questioned whether it was a wise decision to travel 13 hours…each way…by car…with a 13 month old. Even writing this now, it sounds like a disaster waiting to happen. But we found out rather quickly that Nora is a traveling angel!

We left Peru around 10:00 am on Monday and dropped Bailey off at the Vet for his stay at "doggy camp". He wasn't excited. He went through his typical routine…sitting his butt down and extending all four paws as far in front of him as possible, while pulling the leash back with his neck. I'm sure he was thinking of the last time we brought him there, to perform emergency surgery for bladder stones. I likely would have been digging my heels in too.

We left Plattsburgh at 10:30 am, crossed the border, and were making good time until we hit a single lane of traffic, backed up for miles, just south of Montreal. We didn't know at the time, but three trailers collided on the road ahead of us. We sat stationary on the highway for 1.5 hours! Luckily, Kelly and Nora were sound asleep. I took advantage of the stop and polished off a significant chunk of the remaining pages I had to read of the Da Vinci Code.

The rest of the trip to P.E.I. went smoothly. We traveled northeast from Montreal, past Quebec City and on to Riviere du Nord, where we turned south and entered New Brunswick. We passed through Edmundston, Fredericton, and Moncton, before finally catching a glimpse of the Confederation Bridge connecting mainland Canada to P.E.I.

We made several stops along the way to let Nora run around. Most of these little romps took place in Petro Canada parking lots, where Kelly would spend the entire time stopping Nora from eating cigarette butts she'd pick up off the ground.

By chance, one of our rest stops was in Hartland, New Brunswick, home of the world's longest covered bridge. While Kelly nursed Nora, I set foot on the bridge, to stake my claim of having walked on it. I snapped a picture and was then nearly run over by a driver anxious to get on the bridge (it's one lane, and you have to wait if a car is already in route across it).

Nora slept the remaining 4.5 hours of the trip. We arrived at our Bed and Breakfast, The Summerside Inn, at 1:30 am. The owner, Jim, met us at the door and showed us to our room. He, and his wife Jeannie, were more than accommodating, and our stay at their home was wonderful. (Note: Believe it or not, Jim is a Marine and dual American-Canadian citizen who supports John Kerry. His wife told us early the next morning that they don't talk politics because she supports Bush!)

We awoke Tuesday morning to a perfect day. Nora and I went for a 5-mile run along the coast, while Kelly caught up on some much needed sleep. For breakfast, we had fresh blueberries…the best, juiciest, flavor filled blueberries I've ever had. The blueberries here at home aren't bad, it just seems that half of them are soft, bland, or super tiny. Only once in a while, will you get a perfect tasting berry with the right combination of firmness, size, sweetness and tart. Eating P.E.I. blueberries was like eating bowl after bowl of those perfect berries!

Before we went out for the day, we checked the weather channel and noted the forecast for the rest of the week called for rain. We decided we should take advantage of the sun, and drove to P.E.I. National Park in Cavendish. The National Park is located on the northern shore of the island. Its characteristic features are red clay cliffs and rolling, parabolic sand dunes. Visiting in September also gave the added bonus of no crowds.

Nora enjoyed her first visit to the ocean by walking the beach, picking up and throwing rocks, pointing out EVERY bird in the province, and of course, tasting everything she touched. She didn't seem interested in the ocean. I tried several times to place her on the wet, packed sand, where the ocean would creep in with each breaking wave, but as the water approached, she'd turn and scoot away as quick as possible.

Wednesday morning we packed the car and drove to Charlottetown, the capital of P.E.I. It was an overcast day, with off and on rain showers, so it was perfect for the short drive and some shopping. The downtown waterfront area, which reminded me of towns like Portsmouth or Kennebunkport, was full of neat little shops. We bought some birthday presents, souvenirs, and a little food, and enjoyed a relaxing foot tour through the city. While Kelly was paying for some T-shirts, I snapped this quick picture of Nora near an Indonesian Totem Pole.

Kelly and I have attempted to purchase some sort of artwork on all our vacations that we can display in our home. It's our way of remembering and celebrating the places we've visited. This trip, we both managed to find something we enjoyed. As we were still finding our bearings in Charlottetown, we stumbled into a little art studio. Kelly picked out a couple prints by a local artist. Each beautifully captures the unique red clay roads and countryside we viewed as we drove through the province.

One of the other shops we visited was an Inuit Art Shop. They sold hand carved and polished stone figures…polar bears, seals, moose, and Inukshuks. The Inukshuks were what caught my eye. They are piles of stones, arranged roughly to resemble a human figure. They are used to mark trails and in Canada are symbolic of people's interdependence on others.

I have always preferred art that is symbolic of something important to me. When I began hiking in the Adirondacks with my family, we became accustomed to seeing "cairns" along many of the trail-less peaks or barren mountaintops. I always looked for them, and felt comforted by their presence. It was a reassurance that I was headed in the right direction. I never really thought too much about how it connected me to others, but in reading about the Inukshuks, I realized that others put the markers there to make my trip easier. They were helping me.

It was exactly what I look for in art. It captured an experience from my past, was a reminder of a vacation with my family, and symbolized a philosophy I find honorable. At first I hesitated, as the cost was higher than I expected. We left the store, and walked some more, but I knew I wanted to make the purchase. I told Kelly I wanted to go back to the shop, and she started laughing. Apparently, as we left the shop the first time, she didn't have to use the restroom as she said. Nora and I walked away, and she ran back to the store to buy me an "early" Christmas present. I may have ruined the surprise, but I felt good that Kelly picked up on how important the artwork was to me.

Thursday was a quiet day. The weather wasn't great, and we finished up the remaining shopping we had planned. We visited the University of Prince Edward Island, and made a few purchases at the bookstore. It was the second day of classes for the semester, so the campus was swarming with kids. I still feel pretty young, but try walking into any college student center with your wife, carrying an umbrella, and pushing a baby jogger with your daughter. You'll realize quickly that you're no longer young!

Thursday afternoon Kelly and I talked about leaving a day early, as the weather forecast was not promising for Friday. We didn't want to just sit around in the Hotel for a day. We decided we'd make a last minute decision, and see how things looked Friday morning. The rest of the day we spent relaxing in the hotel, which Nora, decked out in her special sweatsuit, found more than entertaining.

It was the best decision we made. Friday morning was overcast, but comfortable, and we decided to stay the extra day, and take another trip up to the National Park and northern beaches.

The National Park has a number of hiking trails, all in close proximity to the beaches, so it was easy to visit both without having to keep putting Nora in and out of the car seat. We found two beautiful trails in Stanhope that wound through Spruce forests and around a small lake. We walked for over an hour without seeing another person. It was one of the most relaxing, peaceful walks I can recall.

After the walk, we crossed the road and spent some time on Stanhope beach. There was never more than 2 other people on the beach the entire time we were there. Miles in each direction, and we had the place to ourselves. It was wonderful!

Nora once again enjoyed the rocks and sand. We picked out some souvenir red rocks to bring home, and played until the rain started to fall.

By the time we got back to the Hotel Friday afternoon, we were all pretty tired. We picked up Greek food for dinner (mmmmm…hummus) and relaxed for the rest of the evening. I finished the Da Vinci Code, and bit my tongue, unable to talk about it as Kelly is now going to start reading it. Nora entertained us until we went to bed and prepared for the long trip home Saturday.

Only one event of note occurred driving home. We RAN OUT OF GAS on route 2 in New Brunswick (aka, the middle of freaking nowhere)! In a town called Standish, we passed a sign saying "last chance for gas for 70 km". I suggested we stop, but the baby was asleep, and we didn't want to chance waking her up. Besides, we had more that a quarter tank remaining.

We quickly found out that what makes parts of Canada so appealing (lack of crowds and beautiful country) is also what makes parts of Canada feel like you're living in the 1800's! We passed exit after exit, well beyond 70 km without so much as a convenience store. Nothing. Finally, 10 miles further than Kelly's car had ever gone without refueling, we saw a sign for gas 2.5 km away. We made it, and exited, but once again, no gas! We even traveled a good 5 miles each way…holding our breath the entire time…with no sign of a station. We now knew we were in trouble. Without a better option, we pulled back on the highway and hoped for the best. Not long later, the old RAV4 started to sputter, and I hit the hazards and let us coast as far as possible. If I was going to have to run to the next gas station, I was going to limit the distance I had to travel by as much as possible.

Thanks to Kelly's Mom's cell phone, which we borrowed just before we left, we only lost about 45 minutes and $50 Canadian. The rest of the trip went smoothly, and we were home by 10:30 pm.

I don't like to rate vacations…they all have their highs and lows, but I have to say this was one of our most enjoyable vacations. Having Nora with us amplified our enjoyment of everything we did. Watching her on the beach…exploring the hotel room…chasing birds…eating fish for the first time (while flirting with the waiter)…sleeping between us like a little angel…yelling "Jake" at *every* dog that walked by.

I can't imagine anything more enjoyable.

September 21, 2004

<u>#1</u>

In darkness aft the door an angel slept,

Night's moonlight shone to trace her tiny frame,

The happiness within her heart accepts,

The love her parents make their only aim.

No longer does she nap atop my chest,

Where warmth and heart consoled her tired lids.

Those days I know confirm I'm truly blessed,

That bond, a gem, whose shine cannot be hid.

The rose grows tall as sun and rain provide,

And too an angel buds her precious wings.

She learns by bounds, the seasons change outside,

Each day new thoughts give rise like sprouts in spring.

And though our gut would like to freeze the day,

Our sense of freedom lets her chart her way.

September 30, 2004

Marathoning Leaders

The new issue of Runners World was delivered to my house last night. One particular article caught my eye…it dealt with our political leaders and their marathon careers. We've all heard George Bush has run 3:44…and John Edwards has actually run 5 marathons, including a 3:30 in 1983.

But what I found the most reflective of all the candidates was John Kerry's claim that he ran the Boston Marathon! He says he ran sometime in the 70's, and doesn't remember his time. Ha! Even better, there is no documentation that he ever even *participated* in Boston!

I think that's just fitting for someone who so desperately wants to stand for something…but has never actually *proven* he can *do* anything.

October 01, 2004

A Lesson Learned

Bailey is 6 years old.

Over the course of his six years he's taken several walks a week with us, and has been introduced to countless dogs. Dogs of all types.

Rottweilers, Labs, Poodles, Yorkies, Retrievers, Terriers, even an Afghan on the beach in Maine.

And though he's kind of neurotic, he's found a way to get along with all of them.

Except Baxter.

Baxter is a mutt who runs free in the neighborhood. He's friendly enough, *to your face*, but you know he's causing you trouble when you're not looking. For some reason, Bailey doesn't like him. He's the only dog Bailey will actually show his teeth to.

Baxter runs around him, hopping playfully…but if he gets too close, Bailey flips up his lip and lets out a snarl.

When we moved to our neighborhood, just about every walk had a least one incident with Baxter. He was the Top Dog, and used his freedom and muscle to try to control Bailey.

But Bailey stood his ground. He was smaller, and on a leash, but was confident in who he was. And without a real confrontation, he wore Baxter out.

Our walks are more peaceful now, and Bailey has made new friends. Chewy, Sailor, Socks, Roenick, CJ…

No more headaches caused by one oddball.

Bailey moved past the mutt and is better off today because of it.

October 06, 2004

Vice Presidential Debate

All my political geekery is about to unfold before you.

The Vice Presidential Debate last night fantastic!

As a whole, it was the most enjoyable debate I can remember. The event flew by like an engrossing movie, and I don't remember a single, dull moment.

And now I think the country has a clear picture why President Bush picked Dick Cheney.

He exudes confidence.

Credibility.

Control.

In a word, he was *Presidential.*

In only 90 minutes, he systematically picked John Edwards apart, chewed him up, and spit him back out at Gwen Ifill's feet. Without raising his voice, or even furrowing an eyebrow, he calmly, patiently exposed Edwards as the sniveling, slick, trial lawyer we all knew he was.

It seems a fundamental point, but when you're participating in a debate, you need to answer the questions. Edwards' answers were always framed in the context of what Bush and Cheney have done wrong. He is very good at criticizing, but ask him for a genuine creative idea, and he can't give it to you. Yes…I did hear him say "John Kerry and I have a plan", several times throughout the debate, but never anything concrete to back it up.

Style versus substance. Kerry and Edwards are trying to appeal to the country's emotions. They want you to get mad at President Bush. They say they'll do better, but won't (and can't) tell you how they'll do it. We're starting to see that behind all the talk, there's nothing there. Empty words, and no heart.

I think the most piercing point that Cheney made was when he pointed out that as President of the Senate, he had never met John Edwards. Edwards claims to be able to build a coalition, bring people together, unite differing opinions, yet he doesn't have the time as a freshman Senator to walk up the aisle and introduce himself? How can he even think of bringing the two sides together when he's not even willing to speak to them?

Cheney summed up his opponents perfectly. "Whatever the political pressures of the moment requires, that's where you're at."

Stick your finger in the air, John Kerry.

Dick Cheney built a brick wall, and your momentum train just crashed into it.

What are you going to change this time?

October 18, 2004

Politics

My political career began and ended when I was in sixth grade.

Like many elementary schools across the country, we had class elections. It was an exciting way to learn how our government worked. Anyone who wanted to run for office (President, Vice President, Secretary, or Treasurer) was able to sign up and participate. The only requirements our teacher imposed were that we each had to address the class, make campaign posters to hang throughout the school, and participate in a debate.

I decided to run for Vice President. I was terrified about giving a speech *in front of other people*, but I wanted the job. Ronald Reagan was elected President the previous year, and I had a newfound excitement with anything political. I thought I could make a difference.

Vice President was the position for me. I could share my ideas, and was willing to work, but I wouldn't have to be the voice of the class. I thought I could work quietly behind the scenes.

I never got the chance.

I got creamed in the debate.

My platform was built on trying to get an extra 15-minute break in the morning and more of the hour-long Disney Science movies we all liked so much. I had spoken to our teacher and received verbal agreement on both issues *before* Election Day! How could I fail? The promises I made were guaranteed to happen.

That's when I was introduced to the nasty side of politics.

In his opening statement, my opponent, Charlie, promised our class, full of sugar loving 12 year olds, a soda machine! It wouldn't be placed in the cafeteria, or on the playground...*it was going to be a soda machine for our classroom!*

I was horrified. How could I compete with a never-ending supply of Mountain Dew only inches away from our desks? And how did Charlie manage to swing such a deal? Our teacher scowled when kids drank soda on field trips, and he was going to let Charlie put a machine in our class?

The debate was a nightmare. Each time I attempted to talk about my platform, the follow-up questions were always, "Well, what about the soda machine?" Charlie sat there with a smug look on his face. He won the election with the first sentence of his opening statement.

It didn't matter to Charlie that it wasn't reasonable to put a soda machine in our classroom. He never even checked with the school to see if it was possible. He made the promise because he knew that's what everyone wanted to hear. I tried my best to point out that the school wouldn't allow it, and that if Charlie were elected, everyone would be disappointed, but it didn't work. My classmates were blinded by Charlie's exciting campaign promise.

Charlie won in a landslide. The very next day, he asked our teacher where he could put the machine, and was given an answer he didn't expect. Our teacher explained to Charlie that the school had rules about vending machines, and where they could be placed. Unsatisfied, Charlie appealed to the Principal. But the response was the same.

Charlie spent the remainder of sixth grade (and actually all through high school), relentlessly being hounded about his campaign promise. And kids can be rough.

I think he learned his lesson.

I too learned a lesson. I learned that running for political office will bring out the worst in some. I learned that promises aren't always kept…and that some aren't even possible!

We're now in the middle of one of the closest Presidential contests in our country's history. I see one candidate who answers questions based on experience. Experience he gained in office. And I see a challenger who answers questions by promising the stars. He promises health care, no tax increases, better education, more troops, tort reform, better jobs, better pay…the list is endless.

Sounds to me a lot like sixth grade.

Big promises.

But choose wrong, and we'll all be lined up in the hallway at the water fountain.

0-595-33808-9